The Trauma & Adversity Workbook For Teens

Mindfulness-Based Skills To Overcome & Recover From Prolonged Toxic Stress

Gina M. Biegel, MA, LMFT
Stacie Cooper, PsyD

16pt

Copyright Page from the Original Book

Publisher's Note

This publication is designed to provide accurate and authoritative information in regard to the subject matter covered. It is sold with the understanding that the publisher is not engaged in rendering psychological, financial, legal, or other professional services. If expert assistance or counseling is needed, the services of a competent professional should be sought.

INSTANT HELP, the Clock Logo, and NEW HARBINGER are trademarks of New Harbinger Publications, Inc.

New Harbinger Publications is an employee-owned company.

Copyright © 2023 by Gina M. Biegel and Stacie Cooper
Instant Help Books
An imprint of New Harbinger Publications, Inc.
5674 Shattuck Avenue
Oakland, CA 94609
www.newharbinger.com

All Rights Reserved

All artwork herein remains the copyright of Gina Biegel and of Stressed Teens.

Interior illustrations by Breanna Chambers

Acquired by Jess O'Brien

Edited by Karen Schader

Library of Congress Cataloging-in-Publication Data on file

TABLE OF CONTENTS

Foreword	vii
Section I: Your Go-To Trauma and Adversity Toolbox	1
What's in Your Toolbox	2
Welcome Yourself to This Moment	6
Things in This Moment: TITM	9
Keeping Safe	19
Navigating This Book	24
Section II: Your Life Experiences: Toxic Stress, Adversity, and Trauma	28
1: the backstory on pain and stress	29
2: how stress affects your functioning	35
3: toxic stress and your safety	44
4: your adverse youth experiences (AYEs)	49
5: your lifeline: the timeline of your life	58
6: your adversity response	65
7: how resources impact health positively	71
8: dive deeper: the impact of trauma in your life	76
9: responses to trauma	81
10: negative coping and self-harming behaviors	87
11: not having resources hurts your health	93
Section III: Navigate Your Adversity: Resource Yourself with Mindfulness-Based Skills	101
12: the power of mindfulness: responding and reacting	102
13: reactions to trauma and stress: your nervous system in action	110
14: identifying your rocks: the things weighing you down	119
15: your relaxation toolkit	127
16: your brain in action: taking in the good	131
17: grounding yourself: calm and connect	135
18: choice awareness: the actions you take and the choices you make	142
19: managing your anger constructively	148
Section IV: Pivot and Start Again: Growing Through Adversity	156

20: setting healthy boundaries	157
21: engaging in self-care to be there for yourself	164
22: cultivating your gratitude garden	172
23: your past does not define your future	180
24: letting go and forgiving	186
25: treating yourself with compassion	193
26: building your tribe: finding those you can trust	199
27: one day at a time: drop your rocks to lighten your load	206
28: the bank of well-being	213
29: resourcing yourself	221
30: controlling the controllables	224
Safety Check	231
I Need Immediate Assistance Right Now	232
References	238
Back Cover Material	244

"Gina Biegel is one of the world's leading experts on helping teenagers manage stress and grow resilient well-being. In this wonderful book, she offers a super-practical tool kit along with her personal stories and tremendously caring and nurturing heart. Highly recommended!"

—**Rick Hanson, PhD,** author of *Making Great Relationships*

"Gina Biegel and Stacie Cooper have created a wise, caring, and helpful guide for any teen who has experienced significant adversity in their lives. Filled with clear explanations of cutting-edge ways of understanding trauma and the threat states of mind it can create, this important book helps the adolescent reader to identify overwhelming experiences that have stressed their ability to cope well, and the persistent shadows that cast darkness in daily life. Clear steps to noting understandable but now unhelpful ways of dealing with these adversities are then followed by practical tools to build life-affirming skills of thriving. Hope and healing are just moments away in this fabulous manual to move from struggling with trauma to living freely and fully with strength and joy."

—**Daniel J. Siegel, MD,** *New York Times* bestselling author of *Brainstorm* and *IntraConnected*, clinical professor at UCLA School of Medicine, and executive director of Mindsight Institute

"Life can be challenging at times to navigate, especially when you're a teenager. While I wish

I had *The Trauma and Adversity Workbook for Teens* as a resource as a young girl, I'm happy that this is a tool that is available today. It's practical, easy to navigate, and immediately applicable in moments of crisis and introspection alike. The graphics, exercises, and bite-size chunks help to simplify big concepts and make them less overwhelming. It's a portable trauma tool kit. As a parent, I'd recommend this invaluable compendium of resources to anyone with a teenager because learning to navigate trauma and adversity early in life is something that will carry a child into a more navigable future throughout every decade of their existence."

—**Shelly Tygielski,** founder of Pandemic of Love, and author of *Sit Down to Rise Up*

"A beautiful and connective energy weaves its way through the pages of the workbook, helping young readers feel seen, supported, and encouraged to remember that they are not alone in their life's journey. Biegel and Cooper share practical, applicable knowledge in a way that feels just as authentic, protective, and empowering as the treasured advice of a wise and loving older sibling."

—**Sharon Salzberg,** author of *Lovingkindness* and *Real Life*

"A powerful, empowering guide to personal growth and recovery. Gina Biegel lays out a clear path with many useful tools for self-regulation, self-awareness, and self-growth."

—**Christopher Willard, PsyD,** faculty at Harvard Medical School, and author of *Alphabreaths*

"I have known Gina Biegel for nearly a decade and her work has been a resource in supporting my patients. She has dedicated her career to teaching teens to understand the impact of their experiences, their emotions, and their desires on their actions, while empowering them to be mindful and intentional in how they respond to their world. This book is a deeply personal work inspired by years of study, experience, and further enriched by Stacie Cooper's knowledge. It sensibly teaches adolescents to acknowledge, navigate, and grow through adversity. I will be adding this book as a key resource for the teens I work with."

—**Daniel Emina, MD,** child, adolescent, and adult psychiatrist; associate medical director at Amen Clinics Inc.; and coauthor of *The Suicide Solution*

"Gina Biegel's decades of strong work with adolescents and trauma are reflected in her excellent new workbook's innovative organization and wise content. It is a workbook for and about teens that meets them where they are with love, intelligence, and practical tools to help adolescents heal from adverse childhood experiences (ACEs) and successfully navigate an increasingly complex and ever-changing world."

—**Susan Kaiser Greenland,** author of *Mindful Games, The Mindful Child,* and *The Inner Kids Model*

"Gina Biegel and Stacie Cooper are a great resource for teens and mental health professionals who work with teens and young adults. *The Trauma and Adversity Workbook for Teens* is one of their best, with easy-to-understand explanations of trauma and its impact on our everyday life, combined with evidenced-based tools and techniques that young people can teach themselves or practice with their therapist. Looking forward to adding it to my library and sharing with others!"

—**Susan Parmelee, LCSW,** founder and executive director of the Wellness & Prevention Center, which provides mental health support for youth and their families

"Gratitude to Gina Biegel and Stacie Cooper for writing this practical, and clearly written and illustrated workbook for adolescents experiencing adversity and prolonged toxic stress. This empowering and helpful guide arrives not a moment too soon, as we bear witness to rapidly rising mental health challenges facing our youth. The reader is provided with valuable, easy-to-understand information about trauma and toxic stress, as well as engaging practices and activities, including a comprehensive, inclusive, and socially relevant adverse youth experiences inventory intended to promote awareness and insight into their own experiences with adversity.

Encouraging a curious and warmhearted attitude, the workbook is a rich resource of tools to help the reader develop their own toolbox of skills to promote safety, adaptive coping, self-compassion, healing, growth, and resilience."

—**M. Lee Freedman, MD,** child, youth, and family psychiatrist; and coauthor of *The Mindful Teen Workbook*

G.M.B., age 5—Gina Biegel

To all the strong women in my life who have supported me—Stacie Cooper

We would like to take this opportunity to offer our sincerest gratitude to Dan Siegel for his thoughtful review of this book and the useful feedback he provided.

Foreword

If you're reading this book, you probably don't need me to tell you that trauma and adversity among teens has reached such a degree of prevalence and intensity that the situation might be considered a crisis.

You've probably already heard that it's more and more common for teens to be living with the lingering effects of some adversity, whether from their childhood or preteen years. Indeed, recent research puts the prevalence of trauma among teens at nearly 1 out of 2.

You probably already know that trauma can lead to extraordinary harm, not only in its immediate aftermath but also later in life. Indeed, research has shown that adverse childhood experiences (ACEs)—negative experiences among children that may be traumatic—are especially common among girls and racial or ethnic minority groups. And this is especially troubling because, as the Centers for Disease Control has noted, such experiences have been shown to correlate with a range of disadvantages later in life, from higher incidences of chronic health problems to mental illness and substance misuse.

But what you may not know is this: there *is* a pathway toward healing from traumatic experiences, one that has helped many teens and even adults become more grounded in the potential for well-being, more capable of feeling safe and connected in positive relationships, more engaged in their lives with a sense of meaning and purpose.

I know this not only because experts and a growing body of research confirms it to be so. I know this because it's been true in my own life. As a young girl, I experienced growing up in a household in which alcoholism (my father's) routinely led to domestic violence. After my biological parents divorced (I would never see my father again), my mother remarried, and I once again experienced life in a home headed by an alcoholic—this time, my stepfather, from whom I experienced sexual molestation from the ages of nine to thirteen. I was afraid to report to anyone throughout most of my teenage years.

Notwithstanding these and other traumas, and with the support of a long line of trustworthy teachers and friends, I found a way to lean into my inner strengths and innate gifts, and from there, to make it through. Today, I work as a law professor, book author, mindfulness teacher, and public speaker. I'm living a life I could only imagine for myself from the vantage point of those painful childhood years. And the reason is that I found access to the kinds of supportive teachings and practices this book will reveal to you, and I made the commitment to myself to explore, learn from, and grow through them.

In these pages, you'll find lessons on how trauma affects the body, and what you can do to handle its harmful effects. You'll find page after page of practical teachings and exercises to help you move from distress to centeredness, from coping to thriving, and from floundering to flourishing. Of course each of us is different, so don't be surprised if some of the practices or teachings resonate more than others. Just promise yourself to give them a try and give yourself the chance to see what positive possibilities might emerge for you as a result.

But perhaps most importantly, you'll find loving support for your own journey to healing and hope. Along the way, you'll learn the means of becoming your own best, wisest, and most loving friend, capable of the inner skills we all need to navigate the seas of change and challenge that any of us may face.

May you find among these pages the very support you need, and may you be forever strengthened by it.

Yours, with love and hope!
—Rhonda Magee, MA, JD

Section I

Your Go-To Trauma and Adversity Toolbox

You Can Overcome and Recover from Prolonged Toxic Stress, Adversity, and Trauma

2
What's in Your Toolbox

Painful experiences are part of life; they're also real, actual, and factual, but you don't have to let your past weigh you down as if you were carrying a big backpack of heavy rocks. Instead of letting these adversities control your life, you can learn to accept and grow from them. You aren't the things that happened to you—you're who you define yourself to be. At every moment, you can decide what actions to take and whether to respond rather than react.

The activities in this book provide an opportunity to discover more about yourself and how your past adversities have impacted who you are right now. Some include materials you can download at http://www.newharbinger.com/47971.

The four sections of this book are designed as a road map to help you overcome and recover from prolonged toxic stress, adversity, and trauma.

Section 1 Your Go-To Trauma and Adversity Toolbox

Whenever you feel cruddy, yucky, miserable, feeling the feels, and just not quite yourself, you can turn to this section, which focuses precisely on things to do in the moment to keep you safe.

It contains tools and skills to use if you need a quick reset. You'll also find supportive skills on the pages with the following callouts.

Section II Your Life Experiences: Toxic Stress, Adversity, and Trauma

This section helps you explore the toxic stress, adversities, and trauma you may have experienced or are experiencing. Identifying, gaining perspective on, and uncovering life experiences—both past and present—can help you grow, change, and heal.

Unearthing this information can be challenging when it involves hard topics like stress, adversity, and trauma. As you reveal and explore things that were quite possibly out of your awareness until you were explicitly asked, you might notice yourself feeling drained, tired, a bit emotional, and even raw. This is normal. Having healthy tools to mitigate and manage these feelings and experiences is important, and the remaining sections of the book focus on this.

Section III Navigate Your Adversity: Resource Yourself with Mindfulness-Based Skills

Once you have increased awareness and insight around your life experiences, you might be wondering, *Now what?* This section focuses on mindfulness-based skills to help you navigate what you've learned about yourself. You can look at this section as "emotional first aid" to help you cope with and work to manage the stress stemming from your life experiences.

Section IV Pivot and Start Again: Growing Through Adversity

Although it can be hard to change, awareness can provide you with new opportunities to grow. Every moment is an opportunity to pivot and do something different.

This section focuses on ways to move forward, to shift away from the tendency people have to add to their pain and make their overall suffering worse. To push against the tendency to stay stuck and instead to put you in the driver's seat and in control of your life. It helps you consider new perspectives and identify where you need to make changes and do things differently. You'll learn ways to use experiences in your life that benefit your well-being. The section provides you with a path to continue to move forward and release the emotional rocks you've been carrying—to step outside the shadow of your pains, adversities, and traumas.

It bears repeating: You are not defined by the adversity and trauma you've endured. You are not the things that happened to you. You are who you define yourself to be.

Mindful Takeaway

At the end of each activity, you'll find a mindful takeaway. These are quick points we consider key information for a given activity. They may include a sentence to help sink in a point, or they may ask you to do something that can help make an activity more useful and valuable to you.

Welcome Yourself to This Moment

Mindfulness is about paying attention to your life as it unfolds moment to moment. Every moment is a new opportunity to start fresh, to lessen the intensity of those things weighing you down. You can live your life in each moment as it is occurring. At this very moment, you can choose to start your day over. You don't have to give those stressful life moments and adversities more attention than they deserve. It doesn't mean you aren't experiencing them; otherwise you wouldn't be reading this book. What it does mean is that you can work toward deciding how much mental energy and effort you give them.

Stress, adversity, and challenges are part and parcel of life, but you can learn to let go of that which doesn't serve your health and well-being. We want you to free yourself from those things weighing you down, so that you learn to use your brain to attend to the things that benefit you and to spend less time on the things that take their toll on you—both mentally and physcially. It isn't about forgetting; it is about freeing yourself from the things in your life that have caused stress, adversity, and trauma. We aren't saying those painful moments did not take place, but they don't have to stick to you. You can let go of the past.

You can choose to take in and savor those moments that are healthy and pleasant to you and that serve and benefit you. You get to choose where to put your attention. You can work to lessen the intensity of those painful, harmful, and negative moments. Yes, to notice, understand, work to accept them, and make changes where you can, to decrease their impact on you. It's about working on getting unstuck in the places where you're stuck. It's about freeing yourself.

Like many people, you may cling to your adversity and trauma as a means of self-protection and self-preservation, a way to be on alert so that it doesn't happen again. But holding on to pain can keep you stuck, immersed in past and present wounds.

It's normal and natural to experience and remember one's pain and suffering. Your body provides you with information on how to protect yourself from the same thing happening again. However, people who don't learn to accept, let go of, and forgive often live in pain, shame, guilt, and blame. When they get stuck in their current adversities and their history, they don't get to live their life in the now, as it's taking place.

Knowledge about your past and current circumstances can provide you with a sense of agency, power, and control. It is through knowing that change and growth can ensue. Knowledge without action or change can leave you in pain and stuck. The activities in this book are intended to help you learn, grow, and change—to become unstuck—while easing your stress and pain.

For Inquiry, Awareness, and Insight

Near the end of this book, you'll find a page titled For Inquiry, Awareness, and Insight. At ht tp://www.newharbinger.com/47971, you can download this page as needed to write notes, for extra space you might want for an activity, or for any aha moments or insights you may want to jot down.

As you work through the activities in this book, remember to be kind to yourself and to listen to what you need in the moment. You can refer to the following resources or revisit or skip any of the activities in the book as needed at any time. Our intention is to help you to gain knowledge so you can learn, grow, and make beneficial and positive life changes.

Things in This Moment: TITM

Things in This Moment (TITM) are grounding techniques, safety tips, self-care activities, and suggestions you can use whenever you're feeling activated emotionally and physically by stress, adversity, or trauma—or anytime you want; there are a lot of good everyday suggestions. Use this section to help you in the moment when you need it.

You'll see two different comic-style callouts in some of the upcoming activities. They're there to help support your working through these activities. *If Needed, Go to the TITM Section* lets you know that this activity might be challenging emotionally or weigh on you a bit, and the callout is a reminder to go to this section for an immediate reset. In a few activities, there is a callout with *An Additional TITM Resource*. These activities are full of tips, tools, and skills that aid you in the moment and support your well-being. They're particularly useful when you need mental health support.

Techniques to Ground Yourself

When you notice and focus on different parts of your body in the moment, you're grounding yourself; for example, noticing your feet as you're standing right now, in this moment, is a way of grounding yourself. Grounding techniques are useful when people feel out of sorts, disconnected, in their thoughts more than in their bodies. You can use the following grounding techniques when you need to get more connected to this moment:

- Notice each of your fingers.
- Wiggle your fingers.

- Notice the air or sensations on your fingers or hands.
- Touch a single finger to your thumb.
- Count your fingers.
- Notice each of your hands.
- Notice both hands.
- Notice each of your toes.
- Wiggle your toes.
- Notice what surrounds your feet.
- Walk with your shoes on or off.
- Walk on different surfaces, such as grass or concrete.
- Count your breaths.
- Say to yourself as you breathe, *Breathing in one, breathing out one, breathing in two, breathing out two.* (Do this for as long as you need or want.)
- Notice where you bring air in (your nose or mouth) on the next in-breath.
- Notice where you release air (your nose or mouth) on the next out-breath.
- Notice your stomach rise on the in-breath.
- Notice your stomach fall on the out-breath.
- Notice how your breath moves through your body as you breathe.

Orient Yourself to the Here and Now

Someone who is triggered or activated by a difficult situation, adversity, or a traumatic event, or experiences the memory of these as in a *flashback,* might feel kind of spacey or zoned out. This feeling is a defense mechanism, a way to protect yourself. For example, someone who is experiencing physical harm may tune it out and detach from what is occurring in order not to feel it; this reaction is referred to as *dissociation.*

It's useful to be aware of your surroundings. This list suggests ways to bring yourself more fully into the present moment if you ever feel this way:

- Notice the time of day (morning, night).
- Notice where you are (home, school).
- Notice your five senses (sight, smell, taste, sound, touch).
- Notice your energy level (tired, awake).
- Notice the position of your body (sitting, standing, lying down).
- Notice the points of contact your body has with the surface you're on.
- Let go of any facial expression you might be holding.
- Let go of any clenching in your jaw.

- Release any muscles that might be tight or tense (face, neck, shoulders).
- Notice any physical sensations that are present from the tips of your toes to the top of your head.

Replace Self-Harming Behaviors with Grounding Techniques

There are times when people engage in a self-harming physical behavior (for example, cutting, drinking or drug use, unsafe sex, bingeing or purging of food), in order to numb or avoid an emotional pain. These grounding techniques can substitute for self-harming behavior:
- Be where your feet are; literally look down at your feet.
- Walk barefoot on surfaces such as grass, sand, or carpet.
- Put your feet in cold running water in the tub.
- Walk with shoes on surfaces such as dirt, wood, or grass.
- Hold an ice cube in your hand until it melts.
- Put your hand in or under cold running water.
- Observe each of your hands.

Self-Care in Action Activities

- Get outside and move around.
- Practice mindfulness and relaxation techniques.
- Spend time with an animal.
- Do something for yourself that you often do as a kind gesture for someone else.
- Say something kind to yourself.
- Play one of your favorite positive songs (maybe even dance or sing).
- Take a few deep breaths.
- Laugh.
- Take a nap.
- Exercise.
- Practice a grounding technique.
- Journal.
- Read for fun.
- Write a thank-you note to yourself.
- Write down three to five things you're grateful for.
- Call someone who cares about you instead of just texting.
- Create something, like art, to express yourself.
- Watch the sunrise or sunset.
- Garden.
- Play a musical instrument.
- Look up at the stars at night.

- Cook a healthy meal, perhaps with someone who supports and nourishes you.
- Go on a walk alone or with someone who is supportive.
- Take a short break or step away from someone or something that is stressful.
- Take a bath or shower.
- Smell something pleasant (a flower, essential oil, a spice, a candle, or cologne).
- Play a favorite game.
- Do a kind gesture for someone else.
- Volunteer.

Assessing Your Fundamental Human Needs

Humans have fundamental needs to be safe, feel satisfied, and to be connected. When these needs are being met, you may not even think about them. For example, when you're safe, you don't feel the need to think about your safety. However, someone in an unsafe home environment would often think about how to get and stay safe. Learning how to check in with yourself to assess if you're safe, satisfied, and connected is very important.

Safety

Ask yourself what people or situations in your life allow you to feel a sense of safety. Conversely, what leads you to feel vulnerable, unsafe, uncomfortable, pained, or even threatened?

If you don't feel safe, go to the *Safety Check* in the back of the book to assess what in your environment is causing you to feel physically or emotionally unsafe. If you need immediate assistance, please turn to the section *I Need Immediate Assistance*, which provides resources to contact.

Satisfaction

Ask yourself what people or situations you find pleasant, or are grateful for, happy about, or content with. Conversely, what people or situations do you find unpleasant or unhappy, or make you feel let down, discouraged, or discontented?

Let your answers lead you to those healthy people and situations that contribute more to your satisfaction and less to your discontent. It can be hard when you have to spend time with people you don't feel satisfied with! If you can, spend more time with the people who support your well-being and sense of satisfaction, and give less attention to those who bring you down or don't have your best interest at heart. And spend less time on activities that aren't supportive to your health and well-being.

Connection

Most people need and want to feel connected to others, to be loved and liked. Going through a loss like the end of a relationship, or grief when someone passes, or feeling rejected by another person is hard. These are often the times people feel most alone. Although this is when they most need to be connecting with others, some people do the opposite of what is good for them and disconnect further, perhaps isolating themselves and distancing from people in their lives. Unfortunately, feeling disconnected and lacking connection is almost certain to occur at one point in your life. One way to combat disconnection is to seek out and get support by asking for help. Another is to spend time with people who have your best interest at heart and those you find are supportive to you.

When people feel a sense of loss or rejection, or feel unloved, they may try to fill this void with unhealthy, unhelpful, or even harmful ways of dealing with it (for example, alcohol, drugs, cutting). When you're feeling a lack of connection, please consider those people who are still in your life and those things that you can turn to that support you in healthy ways. As a reference, you can always turn to the list of *100 Healthy and Safe Coping Skills* in Activity 7. At http://www.newharbinger.com/47971, you can also download this list.

Keeping Safe

Here is a quick check-in for self-preservation that can provide you with information that perhaps your needs aren't being met right now and some ways to meet those needs. Ask yourself:

- Am I safe? If not, get and stay safe.
- Am I hungry? If you're hungry, eat when you're able to.
- Am I lonely? If you're lonely, get connected to someone supportive and comforting when you can.
- Am I tired? If you're tired, get some sleep when you can.

The Protective Porcupine: Keep and Stay Safe

One of the most important ways to take care of yourself is to protect your physical and mental safety. The most important thing we want is for you to be safe. First and foremost, protect yourself.

You may think it's selfish to care for or protect yourself—it's actually far from it. You cannot help anyone else if you don't take care of yourself first. Think of this: your heart pumps blood to itself before the rest of the organs in the body because that's what it needs to do to survive. When your safety is threatened in any way, please remember this image of the protective porcupine. You can use the suggestions listed on the life preserver as go-tos to keep yourself safe.

Sometimes in the moment the best way to resource yourself is to protect yourself.

©stressedteens

Engage in Self-Preservation: A key basic human instinct is to protect yourself. It is necessary to protect yourself from harm or danger. Pain and fear are indicators that your self-preservation is in danger.

Ground Yourself: Be where your feet are at this moment. Orient yourself to time and space. Go to the section earlier in this chapter for specific ways to ground yourself.

Do a Safety Check: Ask yourself, *Do I feel physically unsafe right now?* and *Do I feel emotionally unsafe right now?* If you answered yes to either question, go to the *Safety Check* in the back of the book. Go to the Resources section in the back of the book for additional support.

Do a Gut Check: Doing a gut check alerts you when you're in an unsafe situation or about to make a dangerous decision or mistake. Notice if you get a bad or funny feeling, or hear a small voice letting you know that something just isn't right. Notice how you feel in your stomach. Don't deny your intuition or gut instinct. It's better to err on the side of caution if it protects your safety.

Seek Out a Trusted Adult: The best way to know if an adult is a person to be trusted is to ask yourself, *Do I feel safe with this person?* Consider these other questions as well:

"Do I feel respected by this person?"

"Do I feel listened to and heard when I talk with this person?"

"Have I felt positive when I interacted with this person in the past?"

If you can answer yes to at least some of these questions, this person is probably someone you can turn to for assistance.

Things in This Moment (TITM): Utilize the TITM anytime you are feeling activated emotionally and physically. Use the grounding techniques, orient yourself to the here and now, and use the Self-Care in Action activities from earlier in this section.

Mental Health Assessment: Looking for Red Flags

It is useful for you to know some of the common red flags that often alert a mental health professional that someone is having a mental health difficulty. Changes in these key areas may indicate that you need additional assistance.

Eating: Eating a lot more or less than what is typical for you.

Sleeping: Sleeping a lot more or less than what is typical for you.

Sudden mood changes: Feeling more irritable, angry, anxious, or sad than usual.

Interests: Not engaging in the things that interested you before, or enjoying them minimally when you do engage in them.

Relationships: Spending less time with friends and other people in your life than you usually do.

Isolation: Finding that you want to be alone a lot more than you used to.

If you realize that you've had a marked change in one or more of these areas, please

(1) talk with an adult you can trust, and (2) strongly consider seeking out mental health support and services. Refer to the resources in the back of this book if you need help.

We aren't encouraging you to diagnose or treat yourself, or anyone else. We are sharing these red flags because they may indicate the need for you to take action and get additional support.

Navigating This Book

You *can* overcome and recover from prolonged toxic stress, adversity, and trauma! Change takes time. Learning new skills, implementing them, and doing things differently all take time. It's best if you can work through the activities in this book in the order they're presented. They're designed to build on one another, and some are based on skills you will have learned in earlier sections. Doing the activities and using the skills in this book provides you with an opportunity to discover more about who you are and how your past experiences have created the person who is reading this right now. And remember, your past neither defines who you have to be nor determines your future. You define who you are and determine your future by the choices you make and the actions you take.

We ask you to look at the hard things not to make you feel worse, but to learn, grow, and make needed changes to help you feel better and heal where needed. Using the skills in this book can help you learn about yourself. You'll also learn tools to help you tolerate and deal with pain and ease possible challenges. You'll learn ways to engage in self-care, self-love, self-compassion, acceptance, and forgiveness to ease pain and suffering.

Being in Your Comfort Zone

Completing some of the activities in this book might push you out of your comfort zone and asks you to look at things that are difficult. Some pushing and pain can lead to growth and change, but some pain is just too much. Please *don't* push through an activity if you're overwhelmed, flooded with emotions, or feel intense emotional pain—this is far from the intention or point of any of these activities. Listen to your body. If you feel that an activity is too hard right now or pushes you further than you want to be pushed, it is 100 percent appropriate and necessary to stop it and move on to an activity you find less emotionally intense. You can always go back to an activity or skip it altogether. This book is in no way designed to harm you, but rather to help you navigate through the difficulties that have come your way, learn how to manage them, grow from them, and do new things to move forward.

How to Check In with Yourself

We want to be super-duper certain that the activities in this book aren't leading to an unintended negative response or outcome. When working on them, do what feels comfortable; only you know what's best for you. If you get to a point where you just feel overwhelmed or

if something just feels too much, take a pause and check in with yourself. Listen to your body.
- Notice if you feel any uncomfortable physical symptoms. Do you feel nauseous or have butterflies in your stomach? Do your hands feel sweaty? Do you have a headache? Are your jaw or shoulders tense?
- Is your heart beating fast?
- Is your breathing shallow, restricted, or tight?
- How do you feel emotionally? (Sometimes you might not know, and that's okay. Just notice if any unpleasant, painful feeling or emotion is present for you.)
- Does anything just feel off or not right to you?

If you answered yes to any of these questions, you may want to stop the activity for now and work on one that is less troubling for you.

Seeking Mental Health Assistance

The activities in this book aren't meant to take the place of mental health treatment, but they can supplement treatment with a helping professional. Working through some of them might bring up painful emotions or memories that require support. Please explore these issues with a mental health professional or an adult you trust. You can also find some of these resources in the section *I Need Immediate Assistance* at the back of this book.

Section II

Your Life Experiences: Toxic Stress, Adversity, and Trauma

Awareness and Insight Can Lead to Change, Growth, and Health

I

the backstory on pain and stress

for you to know

The human body is fascinating. One of its innate abilities is to maintain a state of balance (aka homeostasis). When your body is out of balance, it provides you with information you can use to bring it back into balance. For example, think about physical pain: you stub your toe. We imagine that just reading these words has brought up your sense of what it feels like to stub your toe.

pain and stress just want to be heard

Pain and stress in your body provide you with information that you're out of balance. Your body is saying, "Hey I'm in pain. I am stressed! Listen to me over here!" There may be times when you're in pain—experiencing a difficult situation—and the stress you feel is not as evident as noticing a stubbed toe, especially when in emotional pain.

Lisa thought she was doing pretty well, going about her day, hanging out in her room, and a song came on, a happy song that she and her brother used to sing when they were younger. She smiled and then got this nauseous feeling in her gut. Her smile stopped. At that moment, she was reminded of something painful that happened a week ago. She had had a conversation with her brother. He shared that he did not have enough money for that month's rent, and their family didn't have the money to help or the room for him to stay. Lisa felt pain, stress, worry, and sadness about her brother's situation, and the song triggered this for her. She hadn't even known it was on her mind or bugging her anymore.

Sometimes people don't want to pay attention to, or deal with, their pain and stress precisely because it is painful. It's normal and natural to push pain away, but over time, pain and stress have ways of expressing themselves. Think about a pot of boiling water: left unattended, it eventually overflows. Over time, the pot can even get burned and become unusable if left on the burner long enough.

Your pain and stress work the same way as a pot of boiling water. Although you might not want pain and stress, or to deal with them, they're a natural part of the human condition. You will have pain. You will have stress. It's what you choose to do with them that's in your control. The resources you have and will learn in this book can help you deal with and manage stress.

On the lines below, take a few minutes to list anything causing you pain or stress. The list doesn't have to be exhaustive; just write down what comes to your mind over the time you have. Here are a few examples: think about the people in your life, school, home, work, disappointments, expectations of others that aren't being met for you.

If you need more space, you can download this image at http://www.newharbinger.com/47971.

something more: manage your stress

A ***stressor*** is generally said to threaten one's homeostasis, or balance—in simple terms, it is something that causes you stress. Knowing your stressors is the first step to help you take action to reduce or change them. Go back to the list you just wrote down, and mark each item:

- Circle those stressors that are short-term, acute, or manageable. With some effort on your part, they will resolve.
- Put a check next to those that are long-term, chronic, and manageable. With a decent amount of planning and action, they will resolve over time.
- Put a line through those stressors that are enduring or unmanageable. Most often these are out of your control because they involve other people or society (for example, Covid-19).

This week, put some effort into a few of the things you circled. Feel some success once they've been resolved, and notice the incremental steps toward managing your pains and stressors. Then over the next week or two, try to work on one of the things you checked. Consider whether breaking it down into steps will help it get taken care of.

Continue to work on the circled and checked items as you're able. New things will arise; old things will go away. If this system works for you, consider using it on a regular basis. And there's another benefit: once you put these things on paper, you don't have to hold on to them in your mind anymore.

Finally, consider how you feel about not being able to change the things you put a line through. Just because you cannot control them doesn't mean these things aren't affecting you, perhaps even a great deal. Since you cannot change them unless other people make changes or something beyond your control occurs, you still have this pain or stress in your life. What you can control is how you respond, and using the skills in the coming activities can help you deal with the more chronic enduring pains and stressors.

mindful takeaway

> **Stress** is the brain or body responding to a demand or threat. Although this definition might seem quite simple, the layers to unpacking how stress impacts health, functioning, performance, and the like are much more complex.

2

how stress affects your functioning

for you to know

Just imagine if your body did not notify you when you were in pain or stressed. There is a proven relationship between pressure (stress) and performance and health (Yerkes and Dodson 1908). Essentially, performance improves with some stress, but only up to a point. Our normal stress response is adaptive and necessary for survival. Because your body's goal is to stay in balance, you get notified when it's under threat, when stress is too great.

human function curve
(aka the stress response)

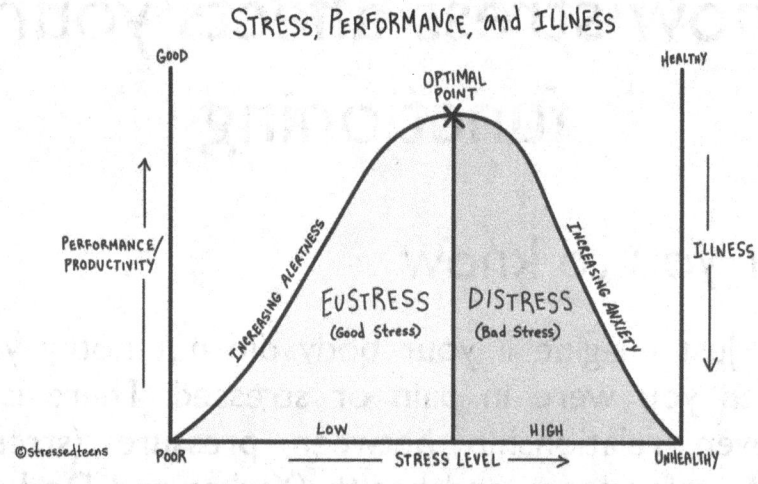

Stress can be both helpful and harmful under certain circumstances and conditions. Look at the stress level at the bottom of the above graphic: as the stress curve moves from left to right, stress increases. The curve begins with low amounts of **eustress** (aka "helpful" or "good" stress). Eustress can help a person be more productive and perform better. For example, eustress can increase alertness and focus. At the top of this curve, there is an optimal point where a certain level of stress helps someone and can provide for peak performance. For example, this is where athletes want to be; sometimes it is referred to as "being in the zone." Take Jamir, for example. *Jamir is about to take a shot in his basketball game. He feels the*

adrenaline pumping, intensity building, and he is alert and focused. The eustress helps Jamir take and make the shot.

When stress gets too high, its benefit sharply declines. Once stress passes this optimal point—a sweet spot, you might say—it turns to **distress** (aka "harmful" or "bad" stress). That optimal point is not fixed or guaranteed. When people get distressed, and their stress is too high, they become more susceptible to mental and physical health risks. Look at what happened to Kesha. *Kesha put off doing a project because she knew that sometimes when she waits stress motivates her to get it done. However, because it worked for her before doesn't mean it will this time. This time, she waited too long to do the project because she was also studying for exams. She didn't sleep well the day before her exam, and she didn't eat very much. This time, instead of stress motivating her, that optimal point shifted to distress, and she felt frozen. She couldn't do the work she needed to do before morning. She couldn't think of any ideas, and the anxiety was getting to her. She kept checking social media as a distraction and pretty soon, it was three in the morning. Not only could she not do the project, she also could not sleep. By the time morning came, she didn't want to go to school, but her caregiver would not let her stay home.* This is a clear example of how stress is constantly in flux and changing based on a number of factors.

Acute Stress

The examples of Jamir and Kesha depict single, isolated events. An isolated event of stress is an example of an **acute stressor,** a common form of stress that generally has short-term effects because the stressor goes away. The outcome might not be what you want, like in Kesha's case, but it resolves at some point.

In the space below, list up to ten acute stressors in your life. You might not think you've had any but think hard; they may be small things like this: *JJ remembers someone startling them because they had their earbuds in and did not know their friend was coming to talk to them.*

Chronic Stress

Stressors that are more enduring, repeated, and long-lasting are considered **chronic.** Generally, continued chronic stress creates a negative impact in a person's life and on their mental and physical health. In the space below, list up to ten chronic stressors in your life. If you cannot think of any, look back at Activity 1.

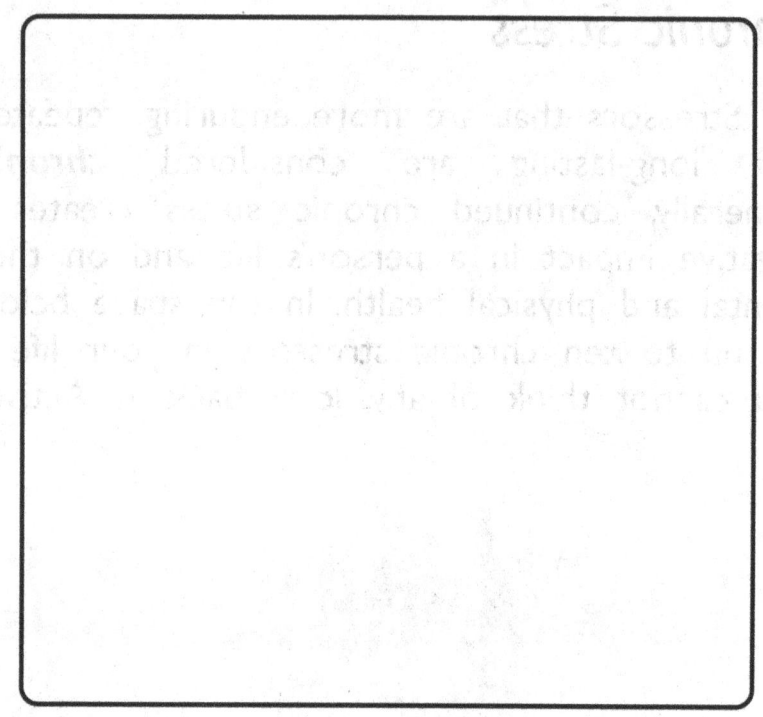

The body responds quite differently to acute and chronic stress. In fact, chronic stress suppresses immune function and can negatively impact your physical and mental health and functioning. Chronic stressors fall into two categories: things that you can change and resolve and those you cannot change no matter what you do. The coming activities will help you tolerate and manage these more difficult chronic stressors.

something more: physical and mental effects of stress

Often people experience different effects depending on the stressor. For example, someone who learns their friend got into a car accident might be much more affected compared to them getting locked out of their house. It's useful to be aware of these possible effects because knowledge can empower you with information about the ways your body alerts you to stress.

This list includes effects you might experience as a result of stress. It isn't exhaustive, and the effects aren't listed in any particular order.

Physical Effects

- Difficulty breathing—shortness of breath or shallow breathing; heavy or faster breathing
- Throat feels like it is closing
- Faster heartbeat—racing or pounding heart
- Dizziness, faintness, or weakness
- Chest pain
- Heartburn
- Nausea
- Change in bowel movements
- Stomachache
- Sweating
- Trembling
- Tingling or numbness

- Headache or migraine
- Muscle tightness and tension
- Increased or decreased appetite
- Change in weight
- Change in body temperature
- Change in sleep habits—insomnia or constant tiredness

Mental Effects

- Worried
- Anxious
- Fearful
- Scared
- Jumpy or on alert
- Nervous
- Hopeless
- Numb
- Isolated or alone
- Overwhelmed
- Panicky
- Restless
- Angry
- Suspicious
- Sad
- Depressed
- Dissociated, spacey, tuned or zoned out
- Unusually pressured or rapid speech
- Worthless

- Hostile
- Frustrated

---
mindful takeaway

When people discuss stress, they usually are referring to harmful stress, but some stress is actually helpful. Even toxic, chronic, and harmful stress is useful because it's trying to provide people with information.

3

toxic stress and your safety

The human function curve in the last activity demonstrates how adaptive and necessary stress is for you to function. **Toxic stress** is prolonged and chronic stress that often stems from adverse circumstances. It can cause negative effects on a person's health and well-being and it is *not* adaptive or necessary for a person to function.

When someone experiences prolonged toxic or chronic stress, especially in their childhood or teen years, this early life stress (ELS) can lead to significant impairment and be experienced as trauma(s), negative physical and/or mental health problems, and even illness and disease. We don't want to scare or worry you, but to educate you because knowledge empowers you.

your safety is a priority

Learning about the toxic stress in your life can help you
- use skills and resources from this book to possibly lessen the short- and long-term impacts of ELS;

- cope and tolerate with the effects of stress;
- learn where your stress is coming from; and
- make needed changes where it's possible and safe to do so.

As you uncover more about yourself in the coming activities, please keep your safety a priority! It may not be safe for you to make changes to the things that are causing you toxic stress if they're part of your social, community, and/or home environments. It is important to:
- make changes only when and where safe;
- use the skills in this book to help ease the impact of toxic stress and adversity;
- refer to the sections *I Need Immediate Assistance* in the back of this book and the *Things in this Moment: TITM* in Section I of the book; and
- look for the callouts throughout this book as additional resources to help in the moment.

We aren't saying you aren't or won't be safe, but if you cannot end something that's causing you toxic stress, consider your safety first and foremost. It's imperative to maintain safety with the people and the communities you're part of (for example, school, home, and work). If anything causes you intense stress when you're reading this book, or at any moment in your life, make sure to consider doing a safety check.

something more: safety check

There are different types of safety. **Physical safety** is being free from harm or injury caused by another person or physical object. **Emotional safety** is feeling safe to be open, to be yourself, and to be vulnerable in relationships.

A safety check can provide you with information about what is impacting your feeling unsafe, whether physically, emotionally, or both. Even if you're safe right now, go through and answer these questions.

Safety Check

Here are the steps to do a safety check:

_____ Are you safe?

1. Who are you with? _____
2. What are you doing? _____
3. What are you thinking? _____

_____ Are you safe?

4. Where are you? _____
5. Why are you in this situation? **Not** for self-blame, shame, or guilt, but if possible, not to put yourself in the same situation again. The why is the context of the circumstances that got you to the current situation.

6. How are you feeling physically? Describe what you are feeling in your body.

7. How are you feeling emotionally? Describe these feelings.

©stressedteens

If you answered no to the question "Are you safe?," please go to the section *I Need Immediate Assistance* at the back of the book.

mindful takeaway

Toxic stress *is not* adaptive or necessary for a person to function. If it's safe to do so, please consider what choices you can make and actions you can take to get out of toxic situations in your life.

4

your adverse youth experiences (AYEs)

for you to know

Stress early in your life, particularly prolonged exposure to toxic stressors, can negatively impact your health. Toxic stressors can come from adversities—those negative events or circumstances that have impacted you or still are. These adversities might come out of your own personal struggles, or from your environment—things occurring within your household, in romantic and/or peer relationships, and in your larger social system.

Adversity is a broad term that refers to a wide range of risk factors: circumstances or experiences that pose a serious threat to your physical or psychological health and well-being. Experiencing prolonged toxic early life stress (ELS) doesn't mean you'll have health difficulties; rather you may be at increased risk of having physical and mental health difficulties. Knowing the adversity you're experiencing or have experienced, and the health risk factors that could happen, can help you with the choices you make and the actions you take now.

Sheila's mom has diabetes. Because of this, Sheila knows she is at a genetically increased risk for getting diabetes. If she learns about diabetes early on in her life and makes behavioral changes, she can decrease the likelihood and risk of her getting diabetes. For example, she can get routinely tested for diabetes. She can work to eat right and exercise.

Sometimes knowing what steps to take is not as easy or clear as it was for Sheila. Also, the adversity might be from your past. By learning about the adversities you have experienced or are experiencing, you can change the things that are in your control. We realize there are some adversities you unfortunately can't change. But throughout this book we will try our best to provide you with as many resources as possible to help you avert the possible safety risks and related impacts to your health.

adverse youth experiences impact health

Adverse youth experiences (AYEs) are different types of risk factors or adversities that take place in one's childhood and teenage years that can have a significant impact. The likelihood is that the more risk factors you have, the greater the adversity in your life, the greater the risk for negative health impact. Having adversity in your life doesn't predict that you will be negatively impacted; rather the exposure to AYEs are risk factors that you want to be aware of.

the adverse youth experiences (AYEs) inventory

A landmark research study published in 1998 looked at adverse childhood experiences (ACEs) and how ten identified risk factors in childhood contributed to the leading causes of morbidity and mortality in adulthood. They found that the greater the number of risk factors an adult had from their childhood, specifically those adults with four or more risk factors, the greater their health risks (Felitti et al. 1998).

The Adverse Youth Experiences (AYEs) Inventory takes a newer look at how your experiences not only in childhood, but also during your teen years, can impact your health later.

Look below at some of the differences between the AYEs and ACEs:

AYEs Inventory	ACEs Questionnaire
Assesses thirty different risk factors	Assesses ten different risk factors
Includes social disadvantages in the questions	Doesn't include social disadvantages in the questions
Focuses on childhood and adolescent years	Focuses primarily on childhood
Newly created inventory	Research and evidence-based
Created in 2021	Created in the 1990s

The AYEs Inventory focuses on thirty risk factors in four different sections, and looks at things that have occurred throughout your entire life. This broader look enables us to explore further a wide range of things that can impact you; for example, social disadvantages.

Section 1 Your Issues

This section focuses on your mental health, identity, legal issues, and challenges that you're directly dealing with or have dealt with.

Section 2 External Abuse

External abuses are those physical, sexual, and/or emotional abuses you have experienced, or are experiencing. This abuse could be by someone in your household, but also includes romantic partners or peers not in your household. This category also includes neglect, both physical and emotional.

Section 3 Your Family/Household System

These are issues someone else in your family or household is struggling with that either directly or indirectly impact your health and well-being. For example, this issue might be domestic violence that you witness or the imprisonment of a family member; the person dealing with the problem might be a parent's boyfriend/girlfriend, a family friend or extended family member, someone renting or living in your house, or a foster parent or caregiver.

Section 4 Your Wider World

You, or your family or household, may be experiencing disadvantages in your community. These are often social problems in the communities you spend time in, including school or access to education, problems getting food, clothing, or shelter. This would also include any legal, political, and/or geographic disadvantages you face.

Read the next few pages, and fill in all the circles that apply to you. A completed circle indicates that you're experiencing this adversity or have experienced it in your past even if it's no longer occurring. It's good that things might no longer be taking place, but your past experiences may still be having a direct impact on you now. Once you've finished, count how many of the thirty circles you marked.

Adverse Youth Experiences (AYEs) Inventory

Your Issues (You yourself are struggling with these issues)

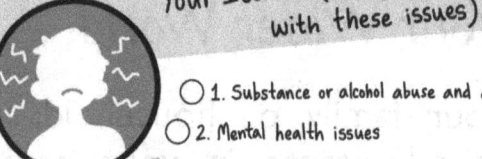

- ○ 1. Substance or alcohol abuse and dependence
- ○ 2. Mental health issues
- ○ 3. Chronic illness
- ○ 4. Aftereffects of a serious accident or injury
- ○ 5. Sexual identity
- ○ 6. Gender identity
- ○ 7. Ethnicity, racial identity, or internalized racism
- ○ 8. Impact of the legal or prison system
- ○ 9. Other disabilities, addictions, or self-harming behaviors

External Abuse (You are being abused by someone in your household, by a romantic partner, or a peer)

- ○ 10. Physical abuse (including domestic or intimate partner violence)
- ○ 11. Sexual abuse
- ○ 12. Emotional abuse
- ○ 13. Neglect (physical and/or emotional)

©stressedteens

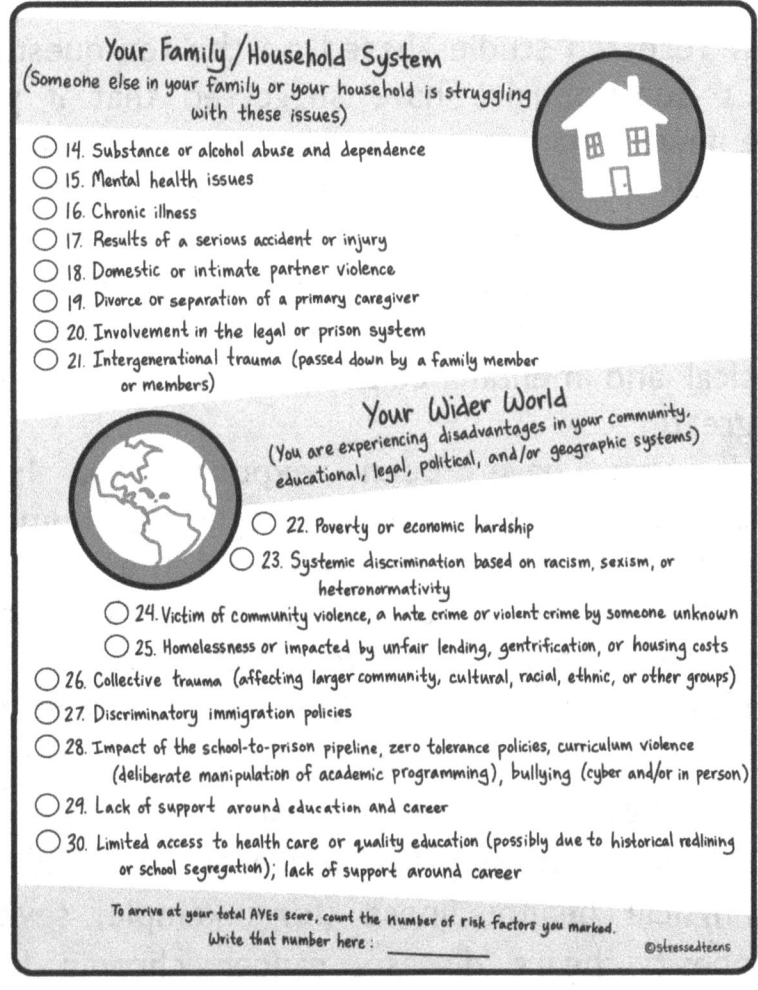

what the risk factors mean: possible outcomes of AYEs

Childhood/youth adversity is linked to possible risks to individual physical and mental health and well-being. There is a strong relationship between the number of risk factors and health difficulties in adulthood. For example, many research studies based on the ten-question ACEs questionnaire have suggested that if you have fewer than four risk factors, the impact is generally less than if you have more than four. Connecting the dots from the ACEs to the AYEs Inventory, if you marked more than four risk factors on the AYEs Inventory, the risk to your physical and mental health and well-being might be greater.

If you have been exposed to, have experienced, or are experiencing a high number of AYEs risk factors, be aware of the possible risks to you. A higher number of risk factors correlates with these health difficulties:

- Health risks for alcoholism and drug abuse
- Mental health problems (for example, post-traumatic stress disorder; depression; suicidal ideation, plans, and even attempts)
- Physical health illness (for example, severe obesity, heart disease, cancer, chronic lung disease, and liver disease)

This list isn't meant to scare you, but to provide you with information.

mindful takeaway

Toxic stress often comes from the adversities in your life. How you experience that stress is not set in stone, and you can do things differently to change the impact it might have on you.

5

your lifeline: the timeline of your life

for you to know

Taking a step back to view the big picture of your stand-out experiences can help you see how they may have impacted who you are today. Writing a timeline of the major events in your life from earliest to most recent can help you do this. In certain contexts, timelines tend to skew to either the positive or the negative, rather than presenting a balance. For example, a timeline of major events during a certain era in history often includes things like battles, wars, and famines. However, when asked to draw a timeline of their *own* lives, people tend to paint an overly rosy picture by focusing mainly on the positive events they've experienced.

The purpose of this activity, however, is to be real and balanced: to encourage you to examine both the good and the bad, the beautiful and the ugly, the joyful and the painful events that stand out in your mind, including any adversity you've experienced.

your lifeline: the timeline of your life

This example shows a timeline completed by Chris, a teen who has been through a lot in only sixteen years on this planet.

Birth: *Born prematurely with twin sister who died, was in the NICU for three months*	
	Age 1: *In and out of the hospital for lung and heart issues*
Age 3: *Mom committed suicide*	
	Age 3: *Moved with dad to a sketchy neighborhood (with high gang activity)*
Age 4: *Dad started drinking more and hitting them and older brothers*	
	Age 5: *Dad got a DUI and went to jail; was sent to live with aunt*
Age 6: *Sexually abused by their aunt's boyfriend during first grade*	
	Age 8: *Older brother sent to jail for selling drugs*
Age 9: *Hospitalized for lung problems for a month*	
	Age 11: *Moved with dad to a small town*
Age 12: *First relationship!*	
	Age 14: *Punched by their significant other and broke up with them*
Age 15: *Transferred high schools due to bad grades and truancy*	
	Age 16: *Made a new best friend and joined dance group together*

On the next page, you will complete your own timeline by filling in each event in your life that comes to mind—whether positive or negative, meaningful or painful (or both)—that impacted you in an important way. Include your AYEs if you want to.

To help you complete the timeline, consider these questions: Looking back at your life, what are the moments that stand out in your memory? What events or experiences shaped who you are, how you feel, what you do, or how you see the world? These specific examples may also help you come up with events for your timeline:
- A family member or loved one's birth, illness, or death
- Your own hospitalization or illness
- A change in where you live or your school
- Starting something new, such as a hobby, sport, or activity
- A significant accomplishment, such as scoring the winning goal in a game
- Your parents' or guardians' separation or divorce
- Unique experiences, such as traveling out of the country or adding an adopted child to your family

- Traumatic or adverse experiences—physical or sexual abuse, mental health problems or addiction of a loved one, community violence, homelessness, discrimination, natural disaster, and the pandemic (those identified in the AYEs).

Now use the long lines to add events to your timeline; for each event, record the age you remember being *or t*he grade you were in on the short lines. You can use a separate piece of paper if there isn't enough room.

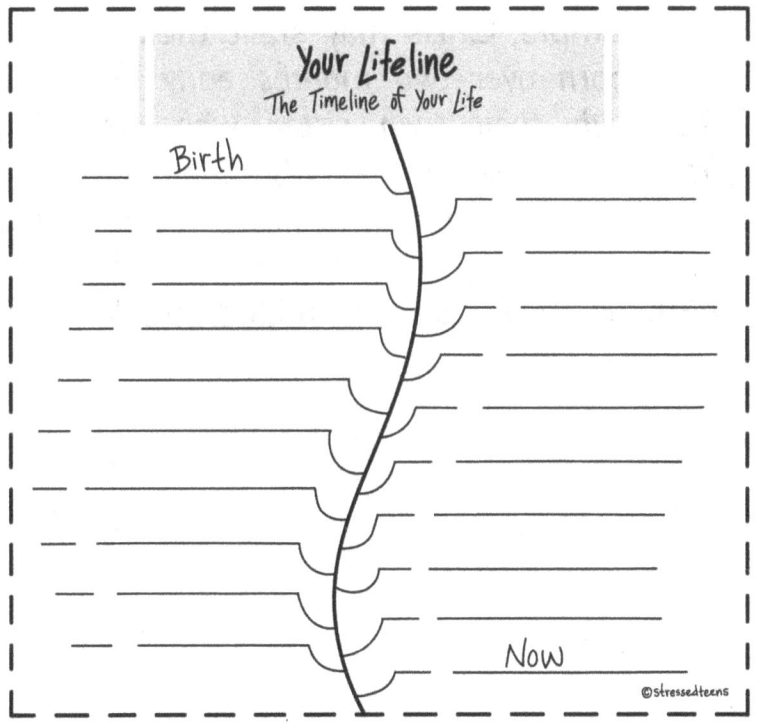

something more: write it out

Now that you've revisited your life from birth to this moment and plotted out the key events, take some space below to summarize them in paragraph form. Try to take a step back and keep your emotions out of it. You could pretend you're a reporter just reporting the facts, or imagine that you're telling your life story in third person to someone as you recall, from start to finish, the major things you've experienced.

For example, Chris may start theirs like this: *Chris was born over two months early on October 2, 2005, with their twin sister, who died during childbirth. Chris stayed in the NICU for three months. They were in and out of the hospital for lung and heart issues until they were one. Shortly after Chris's third birthday, their mom committed suicide.*

63

mindful takeaway

Completing a timeline of your life and reflecting on all the key moments—both the good and the bad, the beauty and adversity—helps you take a step back and see where you've been and what you've been through. Your experiences don't define you, but they're part of your history and contributed to shaping who you've become.

6

your adversity response

for you to know

You can get through, overcome, and recover from adversity. Your choices and actions can greatly impact the effect adversity has on your health. Consider this: you might be surviving, but not thriving! Healthy and safe coping skills and behaviors that support your well-being are resources that can dramatically impact the outcome adversity has on you. The activities throughout this book arm you with suggested actions and skills that can buffer the adverse effects risk factors have on your health.

By learning skills and resources now, if you have experienced a number of risk factors on the AYEs, you can

- increase your understanding of how your stress level, mental and physical health functioning might have been, or are, impacted by the adversity you're experiencing or have experienced;
- where you're able to, make changes in your life to minimize, and possibly end, continued adverse experiences and risk factors; and

- use the forthcoming activities in this book as resources to lessen the impact your AYEs score has on you. (Refer back to Activity 4 to see your AYEs score.)

the adversity response: how resources impact health

Experiencing adversity, trauma, and related risk factors, as identified on the AYEs, doesn't mean your future is determined. This illustration explores how using resources can change the impact the AYEs score has on health.

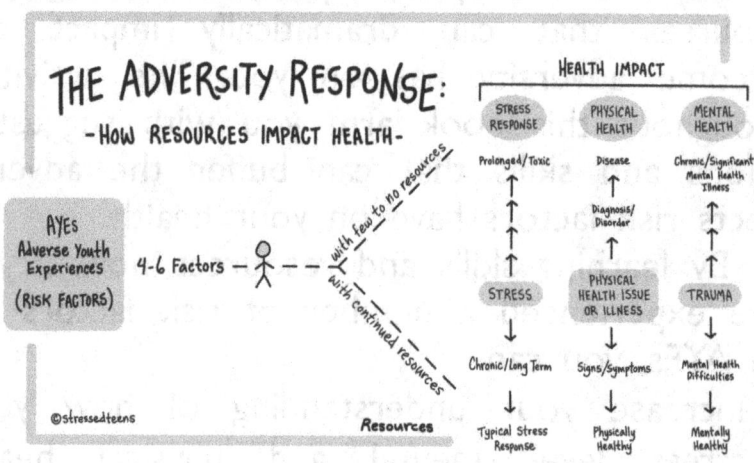

As described in Activity 4, having four or more risk factors *can* greatly increase the negative impact on health and wellness. The person in the illustration above has from four to six risk factors on their AYEs. You can see how their health is impacted by how many resources they have and use. It's important to note that you might have a problem with your physical or mental health that's independent of adversity. For example, a person can have asthma without experiencing adversity in their life.

your adversity response: using your resources

Use this graphic to see how resources impact your health:

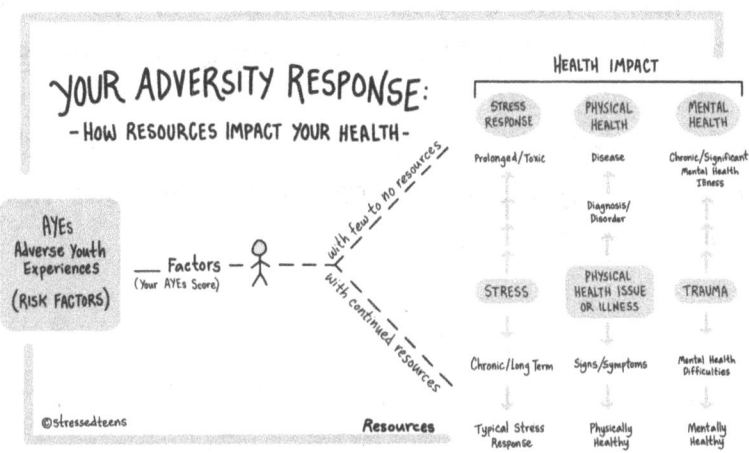

On the blank line before the word "factors" above, write down the score you had on your AYEs Inventory. Under "health impact," the stress-response continuum ranges from the typical stress response (not very stressed) all the way to experiencing prolonged/toxic stress. Where are you on this continuum? Mark an X on the drawing above.

The continuum for physical health ranges from physically healthy to having some signs and symptoms of a health issue or illness to an actual diagnosis/disorder, or even disease. Mark an X to show where you see yourself on this continuum.

The mental health continuum ranges from mentally healthy to having some difficulties, having experienced trauma, or even having a mental health illness. Mark an X to show where you see yourself.

Changing your resources can change your outcomes. Where you marked Xs for these different areas can and will change depending on how many resources you use. It needs to be clear that learning resources and bringing them into your daily life can often improve your health and well-being.

How are you feeling right now? Consider journaling about it if you need to or speaking with someone in your life you feel you can trust.

something more: psychosomatic illness

When you're in a lot of emotional distress, you may have a physical response (for example, a bad headache, asthma, a stomach ache, or a clenched jaw) rather than experiencing feelings such as sadness, anger, frustration, or anxiety, and you may not realize that the physical problem originates from an emotional one. This is often the case with a **psychosomatic illness**—a physical illness or condition that is caused or aggravated by a mental factor, such as internal conflict or stress.

Sarah was getting bad migraines and did not know why. Her sister took her to the pediatrician's office and then to an appointment with a neurologist. After an MRI and CT scan, they could find no physical reason for her migraines. Sarah began seeing a psychotherapist, where she learned that her migraine headaches were coming from a tremendous amount of chronic stress in her home life. Once she worked with her therapist on the underlying cause of the migraines and ways to manage the stress at home, the migraines became fewer and fewer. She also worried less, knowing that she didn't have a more severe medical illness, and she felt a sense of agency that she wasn't just randomly causing these migraines. She felt less out of control. She understood her problems better and felt less like she was going crazy.

mindful takeaway

You might be surviving, but not thriving! Check in with yourself daily and ask yourself, *Am I thriving?* Seek safety when needed; refer to the *I Need Immediate Assistance* section in the back of the book for help.

7

how resources impact health positively

for you to know

Healthy and safe coping skills (aka positive coping skills) are positive mental reminders, strategies, or actions you can take to help support your mood, ease your stress, and manage your problems. Even a person who's experienced significant adversities, even those that result in trauma, will fare better with resources, and decrease the risk for prolonged toxic stress, disease, and illness. It's not to say that someone with significant adversity will have no risk factors for these, but it's likely that resources will positively impact their health and well-being.

resources for you to use

Look over the *100 Healthy and Safe Coping Skills* on the next two pages. When you use any of these skills, you're using resources that can positively impact your health. Mark all the skills that resonate with you, or that you want to remember for later.

Ways to Resource Yourself
100 Healthy and Safe Coping Skills

- [ ] Turn to your grounding focal points (especially when in a stressful moment, feeling the feels, or mentally flooded with a past memory)
- [ ] Drop in to this moment feeling your feet on the ground
- [ ] Orient yourself to this moment: What time it is? Where you are? Pay attention to something in your surroundings
- [ ] Count to 10
- [ ] Replace negative self-talk by repeating 10 times, "I am lovable, I am worthwhile, I am a gift."
- [ ] Touch your thumbs to each of your fingers
- [ ] Wiggle your toes and fingers
- [ ] If flooded by memories from a song, something you smell, and the like turn to one of your other five senses
- [ ] Before making big decisions or responding to something, consider are you HALT (Hungry, Angry/Anxious, Lonely, or Tired) and see if you can change that first
- [ ] Listen to, where safe to ask for, and get, your wants and needs met as often as possible
- [ ] Replace self-harming thoughts, feelings, and behaviors with acts of self-care
- [ ] Ask yourself if the thought you are having is true, real, and factual
- [ ] Talk to yourself as you would your best friend or someone you respect
- [ ] Nurture and treat yourself as you would a baby animal like a puppy or kitten
- [ ] Remind yourself to look for the beneficial things around you right now, even something basic that is benefitting you (e.g., a pen, your phone, clothes you're wearing, coffee cup, the chair)
- [ ] Take in the Good of pleasant, positive, and healthy moments. Attend to them and savor them, let them absorb like water into a sponge
- [ ] Be Teflon to negative thoughts and Velcro to positive ones
- [ ] Resource Yourself with HOT — Have, Open, and Take in beneficial experiences
- [ ] You have to make yourself a priority and put yourself first. It isn't selfish to do so.
- [ ] Take ownership and responsibility where needed
- [ ] Are you expecting more from someone than they are capable of? Work to adjust your expectations.
- [ ] What if it's wonderful?
- [ ] Self-love is your super power
- [ ] Notice what is in and out of your control — control the controllables
- [ ] You can start your day over at anytime, right now, in this very moment
- [ ] Every day is a new opportunity to do something different
- [ ] Cry if you need to cry — it is better to let feelings out than keep them inside
- [ ] Lighten your load, let your rocks go if you can
- [ ] Grief is allowed and helps you heal
- [ ] No one can tell you how you feel, take away, or make you feel something
- [ ] Try to work on the mental hurdles that keep you stuck
- [ ] Be with pain as it is, try not to add to or worsen your suffering
- [ ] Whose problem is it: yours or someone else's?
- [ ] Consider the choices you are going to make and the actions you are about to take
- [ ] Don't mentally beat yourself up; it will solve absolutely nothing!
- [ ] Acceptance can be an answer to your problem
- [ ] Feel your feelings
- [ ] Are you stuck in your story? Start a new chapter
- [ ] Listen to your gut
- [ ] Set healthy boundaries when needed not only with others, but with yourself
- [ ] Take things one moment at a time
- [ ] Pain is here for a reason; listen to it
- [ ] Change takes time, little by slow
- [ ] Get out of your own way
- [ ] Repeat when needed, "I am enough, I am me with my gifts and flaws, and for that I am grateful!"

©stressedteens

- [ ] Repeat when needed, "Allow, release, and let go."
- [ ] Sensitivity is a strength not a weakness
- [ ] It is ok to not be ok
- [ ] Vulnerability is the antidote to shame
- [ ] Self-love and showing up for yourself is one way to engage in self-care
- [ ] Pain can be a touchstone for growth
- [ ] YET= You're Eligible Too, you deserve everything anyone else does
- [ ] Ask yourself are you being H.O.W.: honest, open, and willing?
- [ ] The only way out is through
- [ ] When stuck consider uncovering, discovering, and discarding
- [ ] Gratitude is an action word
- [ ] You can't expect anyone to treat you any better than you treat yourself
- [ ] Don't get attached to the outcome; focus on the hope
- [ ] Expectations are a downpayment on a resentment
- [ ] What you think of me is none of my business
- [ ] Balance a plate; not the platter
- [ ] Accept and appreciate diversity to seek understanding and create meaning
- [ ] Consider safety first
- [ ] Saying no is a complete sentence
- [ ] Spend time with people who nourish and support you, not those who drain and deplete you
- [ ] Every moment is a new opportunity to start over and do something different
- [ ] Just because you did it before does not mean you have to do it again
- [ ] Notice and pivot away from repeating patterns of behavior that are destructive
- [ ] Sometimes FEAR is False Evidence Appearing Real
- [ ] Try being hopeful instead of hopeless
- [ ] Try getting into action instead of doing nothing
- [ ] Celebrate being perfectly imperfect and embrace your strengths, talents, and gifts
- [ ] When needed seek out and get professional help
- [ ] Consider the source of the advice
- [ ] No one will value you more than you value yourself
- [ ] Learn and try not to repeat past mistakes
- [ ] Get yourself out of unhealthy situations and/or relationships
- [ ] Consider the pros, cons, and emotional costs
- [ ] STOP before you act on a thought or feeling
- [ ] Letting go and forgiveness do not mean something did not happen
- [ ] Forgiveness is for you; not for anyone else
- [ ] Negative coping behaviors don't fix a problem, they usually make the problem worse!
- [ ] Pay attention to physical and mental red flags
- [ ] Your values and opinions matter and are important
- [ ] Celebrate incremental successes
- [ ] Pain is inevitable; stress is optional
- [ ] Think of 5 things you are grateful for right now
- [ ] Persevere through adversity or difficult times
- [ ] Your past does not define you or decide your future
- [ ] Walk away from a bad situation
- [ ] Consider those you trust when you need support or help
- [ ] Replace worrying with caring and planning
- [ ] When in self-doubt, fake it until you make it
- [ ] Ask yourself if you are being your own worst limiter
- [ ] There is no such thing as perfection
- [ ] There is nothing good that will come from beating yourself up
- [ ] There is a balance between trusting too many or too few people
- [ ] Be resilient and persevere through the difficulties you encounter
- [ ] You are good enough right now just as you are. You are enough, period!

©stressedteens

Engaging in any of these healthy and safe coping skills can help you when life is showing up, things are getting real, and you're feeling the feels. Also, when you're remembering past pains, experiencing trauma, or thinking about your current stress and adversities, these are the exact times to look at and use these.

something more: your top ten healthy and safe coping skills

Of the skills you marked, which would be useful as a quick go-to list for the future? List your top ten here; then take a picture you can turn to anytime you need a reminder.

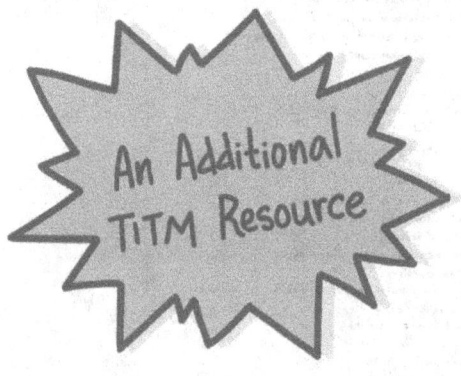

You can also download this page at http://www.newharbinger.com/47971.

mindful takeaway

Use healthy and safe coping skills every day! Remember to review and engage in your top ten healthy and safe coping skills.

8

dive deeper: the impact of trauma in your life

for you to know

Trauma is the result of an overwhelming amount of stress that exceeds a person's ability to cope with, manage, or handle it. Effects of adverse youth experiences can be experienced as trauma. **Physical trauma** is a serious injury to the body—for example, sexual or physical abuse, substance use or abuse, scarring, cutting, or burning. **Psychological trauma** is when one's mind is damaged, impaired, or affected because of a distressing event.

trauma: seen and unseen

You can see a bruise or a scar, but emotional impacts are often deep inside, and because they aren't visible, they often don't get addressed. Take Jaye and Letty for example.

When Jaye comes into class with a swollen lip and a purple discoloration near her left eye, her friend comes up to her and asks what happened. When Letty comes into class, she seems fine, chipper, even talking with people and asking them how they are. What others don't know is that her partner forced Letty to sleep with someone, thinking it would be a good thing for her to do. And even though Letty didn't want to, she did it to stay in the relationship with her partner.

In this example, the impact of intimate partner violence, sexual abuse, and emotional abuse aren't seen. In both examples, someone might be traumatized by their adverse experience.

Knowing what you know can be painful. As a protection, sometimes people don't realize they are, or have been, traumatized because bringing it to their awareness could cause them too much pain and suffering for them to deal with it at that time.

It might seem easier to keep things out of your awareness, to avoid them. However, keeping things out of your awareness, buried deep inside, will often prolong the inevitable: that the trauma, the memories, the experience, and the resulting aftermath will eventually surface, even if you don't want them to. People who don't work to deal with and heal from their trauma often find their long-term suffering much worse than if they had dealt with it earlier, provided it was safe to do so.

get and stay safe

Just as you shouldn't pick at a scab because it will prolong the healing process, you shouldn't pick at a traumatic emotional wound if it's too painful to do so. There's a caveat to working on trauma: Is it mentally and physically safe to? If not, then don't force it! If needed, use the "Safety Check" from Activity 3. Also, refer to the resources in the back of the book anytime you need.

If you realize that you or someone you know is unsafe (for example, being physically or sexually harmed) or if you feel that you want to harm yourself, and the risk is imminent, call 911 *and* go to the section in the back of the book, *I Need Immediate Assistance Right Now*. We would rather you be safe than sorry. We repeat these options to you because we care and want you to get and stay safe.

identifying your trauma

Look back at what you wrote on the *Adverse Youth Experiences Inventory* (Activity 4) and *Your Lifeline: The Timeline of Your Life* (Activity 5). If it's safe to write about them here, which of these do you feel has caused you to feel traumatized?

something more: I feel like crap now

Bringing up and writing about your trauma can cause you to feel your feelings. You might feel mentally or emotionally drained, depleted, exhausted, and the like. Please consider doing something healthy for yourself or engaging in a healthy distraction to ease the emotional pain. Think about how you would be there for your best friend or how you would care for a pet, and apply the same presence, support, encouragement, and love to yourself.

Sometimes people don't realize the way you would treat your best friend or a beloved pet is the way you can treat yourself. If you need ideas, go to the section *Self-Care in Action Activities* in the first section of this book. You might also consider using the journal page at the back of the book. You can download it at http://www.newharbinger.com/47971.

> ### mindful takeaway
> We aren't asking you to open up without ways to be able to close when needed. When identifying, discovering, and uncovering things about yourself and your life, it is important to be gentle and compassionate with yourself.

9

responses to trauma

for you to know

As you read in the first activity, the human body is fascinating. Its endgame is to maintain balance, and it alerts you when it's not in balance. Remember, when you have a stubbed toe, you know it because you feel it physically. However, trauma can be cunning (have skill), baffling (be perplexing), and powerful (impact your life and health). With trauma, to protect itself, the body and mind might not take in certain realities of things that are actually occurring. This is when looking at the ways trauma can present physically and emotionally can help.

trauma and PTSD

People who experience trauma by witnessing a terrifying event can have a mental health condition called post-traumatic stress disorder (PTSD). People who go through traumatic events firsthand can have symptoms that impair their functioning so much so that they might have PTSD.

People who have experienced a traumatic event are said to fare better if they talk to someone and engage in healthy behaviors. If you think you, or someone you know, might have PTSD, please speak to a mental health professional you know and/or use the resources in this book. Doing so can even stop an acute stress disorder from leading to PTSD.

the warning signs of trauma and PTSD

Warning signs of trauma and PTSD can be immediate or delayed, brief or prolonged. Often people who experience trauma and/or PTSD can heal, and often their responses are normal and expected. These responses generally lessen with time and assistance, support, and resources (such as those in this book). Warning signs fall under four different types:

If Needed, Go to the TITM Section

- Intrusive memories: Recurrent, unwanted memories of the traumatic event; reliving it as if it were happening
- Avoidance: Trying to avoid places, things, or people that remind them of the event
- Negative changes in thinking and mood: Feeling helpless or hopeless, losing interest in things they used to enjoy, being detached, or having problems in relationships or trouble concentrating
- Changes in physical and emotional reactions: Difficulties sleeping, changes in eating, engaging in self-harming behavior(s)

This list is general, but not exhaustive.

Is there an event in your life that you've found to be traumatizing? If not, move on to the next section. If so, ask yourself if you have, or had, any of the following warning signs and what that experience is, or was, like for you. Write about your experiences and include what feels comfortable to you.

Intrusive memories: _____

_____

_____

_____

Avoidance: _____

Negative changes in thinking and mood:

Changes in physical and emotional reactions:

something more: subtle ways to identify trauma and PTSD

You may know how you're feeling and what you're thinking, but how you experience trauma may not always be that clear or obvious. You may not know how you feel emotionally, or you may have a feeling that can't be named by the words that people would often use, such as happy, sad, angry, or worried.

Read the following examples of what people report feeling when they experience trauma and possible PTSD. Mark any that apply to you.

☐ Seem blank when trying to think or recall information
☐ More forgetful of what they were just thinking about
☐ Numb, like they have no feeling(s) about the thing
☐ Confused about what's going on
☐ Déjà vu
☐ Spaced out, like they're present and then not to whatever they're doing
☐ Something in their gut makes them feel that something is wrong
☐ Weighed down or just a heaviness to their body
☐ Startled or jumpy when they hear a sound
☐ Exhausted or tired
☐ More emotional than usual
☐ Different feelings than they usually have
☐ A sense that this just doesn't feel right, safe, or okay
☐ Tingly on their body
☐ Their mood is "prickly," like they want people to back off and give them their space

Knowing how to recognize the direct and subtle ways you respond to trauma provides you with useful information.

mindful takeaway

If you feel an intense emotional or physical response, work to orient yourself to the moment. Ask yourself, *What time is it? Where am I?* Pay attention to something in your surroundings.

10

negative coping and self-harming behaviors

for you to know

Negative coping behaviors (aka negative coping mechanisms) are things people engage in that might appear to help the problem or pain, but don't. This is why they're called behaviors and not skills: because they aren't useful in solving problems or easing pains in the long run. Someone experiencing adversity might engage in these behaviors because they were learned from those around them, or perhaps they were the only way they have been able to get any kind of attention, affection, or temporary relief. Negative coping behaviors are also considered, and referred to, as self-harming behaviors because they're often risky and detrimental to one's health and well-being.

negative coping and self-harming behaviors

It is important to look at any of your behaviors that are considered unhealthy, negative, or self-harming. Like many people, you may turn to unhealthy ways to cope because you don't know positive alternatives or because that's how you temporarily self-soothe or manage your feelings. Ignorance is not bliss: gaining awareness of the unhealthy ways you tend to cope with stress, adversity, and trauma is the first step toward being able to consciously choose more positive, healthy behaviors and actions that enhance your well-being and life.

If Needed, Go to the TiTM Section

Read this list of risk-taking self-harm behaviors, if it feels safe to do so, and circle any you're currently engaging in or have in the past:

Using or abusing alcohol or drugs
Isolating yourself by staying in your room
Smoking cigarettes or vaping
Cutting or burning yourself
Carving words or symbols on your skin
Embedding objects in your body or on your skin
Overeating/bingeing
Undereating/withholding food
Making yourself vomit after eating; purging

Exercising excessively
Spending tons of time on social media or gaming
Shopping excessively
Gambling excessively
Sleeping too much or not enough
Stealing
Lying or hiding things
Hanging out with people who bring you down
Not spending time with people who nourish you
Engaging in dangerous sexual behaviors (like sleeping around, having unprotected sex)
Hitting or punching something that would harm you or others
Putting yourself in harmful situations
Pulling out your hair or scratching your skin
Getting into fights
Self-sabotaging (for example, starting fights, pushing people away that are trying to help you)

This list isn't meant to shame you or cause you more pain. Rather, it's here to help you gain awareness of any ways you have been coping that might be harmful to you. Once you're aware, you can start to change your behavior and find healthier and safer ways to manage and cope with adversity, toxic stress, and pain—ways that can actually help. Refer back to the list of "100 Healthy and Safe Coping Skills" to replace one of these.

something more: self-harm tracker

Each time you want to engage in one of the behaviors you just circled, follow these prompts to complete the *Self-Harm Tracker*. Completing the tracker when you have the urge to act is preferable, but you can also complete it after you've engaged in a risk-taking behavior. If you're completing it after, try to write down as much as you remember.
- Write the day and approximate time.
- Describe the situation: what happened, when it was, where you were, who was there.
- Identify the harmful/risky behavior you feel/felt the urge to do.
- Write down any thoughts that arise/arose in the moment.
- Write down any feelings that come/came up.
- Pause. Take a moment before you follow through with the behavior. Notice your physical sensations, thoughts, and feelings.

Write down what you want to do after pausing.
- Write down any new feelings or thoughts that came up as a result.

You can complete your tracker in this book or download a blank tracker at http://www.newharbinger.com/47971. The following is an example of a completed tracker.

SELF-HARM TRACKER

Day and time: Wednesday, noon
Situation: At lunch on campus, my boyfriend said I was being stupid.

Harmful behavior(s)	All I want to do is leave school, hide in my room, take some pills, and numb my feelings.
My thoughts in the moment	My boyfriend is right. I'm stupid and don't deserve anything or anyone good.
My feelings	So many things: I feel ashamed, insecure, sad, angry with myself, and lonely.
After pausing, what comes up	I want to tell my boyfriend how he made me feel and what it triggered for me about my stepdad. I want to reach out to my friend Sam, who is always encouraging. Maybe journaling will help.
My new thoughts/feelings	Isolating and taking pills won't make anything better. It'll just make me feel worse. I'm not stupid just because someone told me that. I'm smart in many ways and have people who love and support me.

SELF-HARM TRACKER

Day and time: _____
Situation: _____

Harmful behavior/s	
My thoughts in the moment	
My feelings	
After pausing, what comes up	
My new thoughts/ feelings	

mindful takeaway

People tend to operate on autopilot, doing what they know, but this can often be detrimental to your health and well-being if you've been exposed to adversity and/or trauma or seen others engaging in unhealthy, self-harming behaviors. Awareness is the first step in taking healthier actions; before you act, be aware. Check in with what's going on within you and around you.

11

not having resources hurts your health

for you to know

Looking back at the Adversity Response in Activity 6, you can see that with few to no resources, stress and health are negatively impacted; this is often because people turn to unhealthy, harmful ways of coping. Beyond self-harming behaviors, people have self-harming thoughts and feelings and can engage in **blocking behaviors,** which are unhealthy behaviors or automatic acts they turn to as a way to tolerate pain and stress. Unlike a bruise that can be seen, these thoughts and feelings aren't as obvious and are often out of someone's awareness.

the relationship between self-harming thoughts, feelings, and behaviors

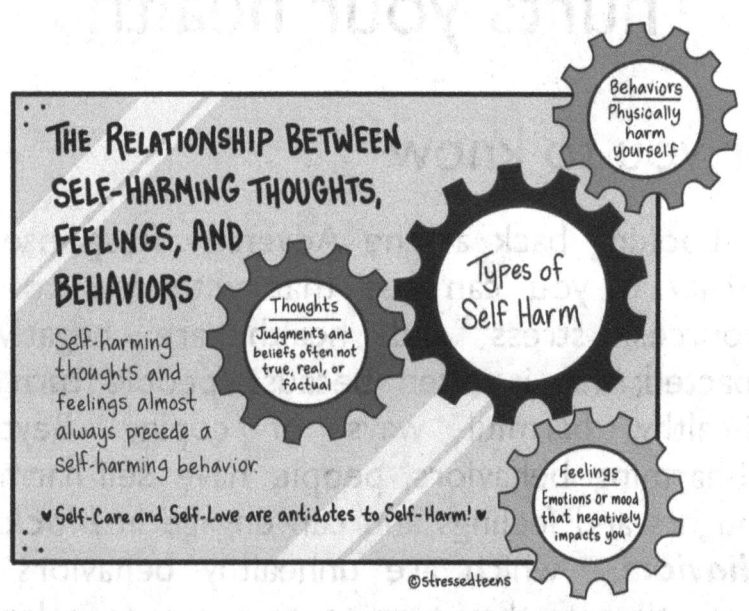

Self-harm is the way you harm yourself physically or emotionally—with your behaviors, thoughts, and feelings. Take a minute to look at the drawing: there are three different types of self-harm. **Self-harming thoughts** are judgments and beliefs you have about yourself, people, places, objects, events, or situations that are not based in truth, fact, or reality. **Self-harming feelings** are those feelings—sad, upset, frustrated, angry, pissed, miserable, overwhelmed, anxious, worried, depressed, and the like—that negatively impact your physical and emotional states and overall health. **Self-harming behaviors** are physically injurious and so are more serious than self-harming thoughts or feelings. Self-harming thoughts and feelings—judgments, emotions, moods, and beliefs—often precede a self-harming behavior.

Self-harming thoughts or feelings are like a car's indicator lights. If you pay attention to those indicator lights—those self-harming thoughts and feelings you have—before they lead to a problem (self-harming behavior), you can begin to do things differently. And if indicator lights aren't attended to, you can have very serious problems.

Note: People can have self-harming thoughts and feelings and not engage in self-harming behaviors. It also doesn't mean someone will engage in a self-harming behavior because they have a self-harming thought or feeling.

What self-harming thoughts and feelings do you have? Write about them here.

[lined writing space]

Look back at "Keeping Safe" in Section I, and consider doing a safety check. You might find a connection between the people or situations that often impact your self-harming thoughts and feelings and trigger the desire to engage in a self-harming behavior.

something more: blocking behaviors: your emotional band-aids

Blocking behaviors might appear to lessen pain and stress, but actually don't. Most often, people engage in blocking behaviors because they don't have healthy and safe coping skills. Engaging in these behaviors can often take an emotional and physical toll on you. Circle any of these common blocking behaviors that you engage in, or have engaged in, when you feel physical or emotional pain:

Denying or ignoring your emotional or physical pain

Pushing the problem or pain away

Socially isolating (for example, pulling the bedcovers over your head to avoid facing the world)

Negative self-talk (for example, *I'm a failure. I'm not lovable. I'm not worthwhile.*)

Feeling guilty or ashamed

Accepting the blame for situations that aren't your fault

Taking no responsibility for situations you have some responsibility for

Denying a problem

Denying what someone has done to you

Not taking needed action steps

Feeling sorry for yourself (for example, throwing yourself a pity party)

Expecting more from someone than they're capable of giving

Minimizing or discounting your own experience or pain (for example, saying "Other people have it so much worse than I do.")

Obsessing about a problem or your pain (for example, by repeatedly checking your ex's social account)

Not wanting to deal with a situation

Avoiding a problem or pain by actively avoiding people, places, objects, or events. (Remember, if it isn't safe, don't engage.)

Choosing not to recognize, or having the awareness of, the adversities or traumas that may be impacting your life

Ruminating about, or regretting, the past

Staying in unhealthy or harmful relationships that you're safely able to get out of

Worrying about or fearing the future

Being stuck in resentments, anger, and hatred

Making your problems worse by actions that keep you stuck (for example, repeatedly playing a depressing song that you know makes you feel worse)

Judging yourself without looking at whether the judgment is true, real, and factual

Telling yourself what you should, could, or would have done differently, or asking yourself, "Why didn't I do that?"

> ### mindful takeaway
> People who don't deal with their problems often turn to self-harming behaviors because they have not identified or worked on their "stuff."

Section III

Navigate Your Adversity: Resource Yourself with Mindfulness-Based Skills

Emotional First Aid to Help You Cope with and Work to Manage Stress

12

the power of mindfulness: responding and reacting

for you to know

Mindfulness is about paying attention to what is occurring as it is occurring. For example, think of your senses. When you notice any of your five senses at a given moment, you're being mindful. Take the example of your sense of hearing: If you've experienced a trauma, noticing and hearing something—perhaps the sound of a door shutting or a certain song—could trigger and bring back memories of when something painful or bad happened to you. Being mindful would be noticing the sound and perhaps also being aware of what else comes up for you when hearing the sound—any thoughts, feelings, or physical sensations.

the power of mindfulness: take a pause

Looking at the illustration below, you can see that when someone is mindful, they're aware of their environment and the things around them (the stimuli). It's in these mindful moments, the spaces and pauses between a stimulus and an action in response to it, where you can be in control and choose what you want to do next rather than to automatically react. Sometimes even a momentary pause can greatly change how something turns out.

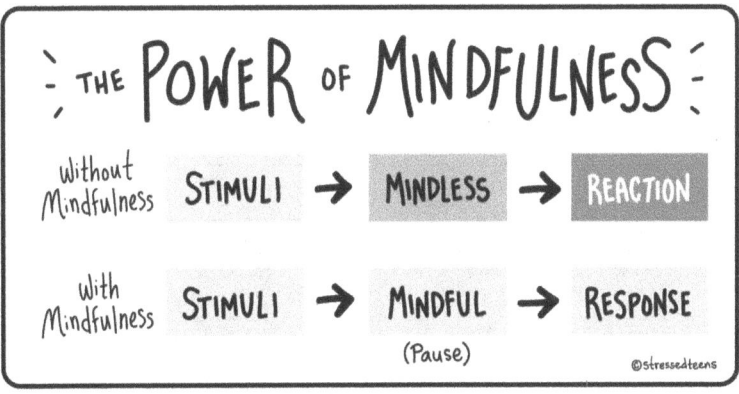

Think about a time in your life when it would have been helpful for you to pause and mindfully *respond,* but instead you were more *reactive.* Where were you? Who were you with? What happened? How did you feel? How did you react? Write all the details you remember here.

What do you imagine, in that specific situation, would have gone differently if you had taken a mindful pause and responded rather than automatically reacting?

While the power of mindfulness is generally in responding rather than reacting, it's also important to acknowledge that there are certain situations in life when reacting is okay, or even necessary. Sometimes an automatic, quick response is protective and necessary for your safety or survival. If someone is threatening you and you don't have time to pause to think or reflect, immediate action might be needed. Consider a time when you protected yourself by immediately responding and acting on impulse rather than pausing and waiting to respond. Perhaps in this situation, you needed to act instantly, either fighting or fleeing, to ensure your physical or emotional safety.

While you don't have the power to control all the circumstances in your life, you do have some power: you can control where you put your attention in any given moment. Being mindful is the first step in taking control of where your attention goes. Once you're aware of your thoughts, feelings, and physical sensations, you can then take a pause and choose what to do next. When you create this space, this pause, you gain awareness of and some power over your thoughts, and thus where you then choose to put your energy and attention in the moments that follow.

something more: mindfulness defined: a short practice

Mindfulness is (1) noticing your thoughts, (2) feelings, and (3) physical sensations in the present moment (4) without harmful judgment. Let's take a deeper dive into this definition.

1. **Notice your thoughts.** Just because you have a thought doesn't mean that it's a fact or real. Think of the saying "Don't believe everything you think." Write down your next three thoughts.

a. _____

b. _____

c. _____

2. **Notice your feelings.** Sometimes people will say, "I think I feel..." Guess what? That's a thought, not a feeling. When asked what they're feeling, most people will respond with a basic one-word feeling (for example, chill, frustrated, bored, nothing, good). Take fifteen to thirty seconds and notice what emotions are present for you right now.

Here are some examples:
Happy
Afraid
Sad
Angry
Lonely
Confused
Excited
Shy
Confident
Hopeful
Worried
Confused
Relaxed

On the lines below, write down the feeling word or words that came to your mind. If you can, give more information than a one-word feeling. Try to fill all three lines. If you can't think about what to write, consider why it might it be hard to notice what you're feeling and to then write more about it.

_____

_____

3. **Notice your physical sensations.** With adversity and particularly with trauma, people might feel physical sensations like numbness, shakiness, or tension. The body holds on to trauma and past experiences. Therefore, mindfulness can be especially useful when managing or navigating your way through adversity and trauma because it increases your awareness.

Scan your body from the tips of your toes to the top of your head, noticing what you can along the way; it might be something new or something familiar. After doing this, write what you noticed in your body.

_____

_____

_____

4. A *harmful judgment* is a type of negative judgment about you, another person, or group of people, that is not based on truth, fact, or reality. *I suck at making friends. I don't know how to stop overeating. I deserve to be hurt.* Now think of two harmful judgments, aka negative beliefs, you often have about yourself, and list them here:

Harmful self-judgment 1: _____

_____

Harmful self-judgment 2: _____

_____

When reflecting on these harmful judgments, ask yourself if there's proof that they're true, real, or factual.

This definition asks you to be mindful of, to notice those harmful judgments you have about yourself and others. It is normal to have harmful judgments about yourself and others. The intention is that when you're more mindful, you will (1) notice these harmful judgments; (2) try to prove them wrong; and (3) work to replace them with more positive, healthy thoughts.

---

mindful takeaway

While you don't have the power to control all the circumstances of your life, you can control where you put your attention in any given moment. When you pause to reflect on what's happening within and around you, you create the opportunity to choose to put your energy and attention in the moments that follow.

13

reactions to trauma and stress: your nervous system in action

for you to know

Imagine you're in a forest and hear a bear roar loudly in the distance. Your heart rate increases, your palms get sweaty, your pupils dilate, your fists clench, and your breath gets shallow. These reactions are your body preparing you to take action to protect yourself. Whenever you feel threatened, the oldest, most primitive part of your brain (called the reptilian brain) tells your autonomic nervous system (ANS) to take action. The ANS plays a significant role in your emotional and physiological responses to stress and trauma, signaling the activation of the sympathetic nervous system to rev up to fight, flee, or freeze. Although you aren't encountering bears daily, you may encounter adversity or trauma-related experiences that activate your body in the same way. Ideally, once you're no longer in immediate danger, your parasympathetic nervous system (think "rest, relax, and digest") puts the brakes on the sympathetic nervous system (think "fight, flight, or freeze"), so the body stops releasing stress chemicals and shifts toward relaxation, digestion, and regeneration. This is what allows you to rest and recover; the ultimate goal is to return to safety.

This activity can be jarring and difficult to read. You are asked to reflect on how you react and respond to stress and trauma. Remember to err on the side of caution for your own mental health, well-being, and safety. If this, or any other activity, feels like too much for you, honor your instincts and perhaps pause and return to it later. As a reminder for this and other activities, when this work feels too difficult, remember that you can go to the TITM section in the front of the book for reminders of ways to calm down and engage in self-care.

responses to trauma and stress: the 5 fs (fight-flight-freeze-faint-fawn)

The most widely researched responses to stress and trauma when you're in self-preservation mode have been referred to as the 3 Fs (fight-fight-freeze), which activate the sympathetic nervous system (*sympathetic dominance*). However, there are two responses that have more recently garnered attention in the research community and are relevant to those who have, or are experiencing, trauma. These responses, the 2 newly discovered Fs, are faint and fawn. Unlike the other 3 Fs, faint and fawn have more decreased or depressed physiological activation (*parasympathetic dominance*). The faint and fawn responses are almost paralyzing, leading to a collapsed state (Porges and Dana 2018).

Yes, these are very technical descriptions, but educating yourself and increasing your understanding and awareness enables you to be in a state of power and control to recognize when you are in a heightened stressful state and in potentially traumatic and/or life-threatening conditions. It's possible to have a variety of responses to stressful or traumatic experiences, and these can differ from situation to situation. When you read about the following responses, think about which ones you've experienced when encountering traumatic events, adversity, or stress, or when you have felt unsafe, isolated, or disconnected.

The **fight** response involves a more aggressive or assertive approach—fighting back against whatever or whoever is perceived as threatening. The fight response typically involves things like feelings of anger or rage; a desire to punch, kick, stomp, or break something; crying; clenched jaw or fists; an upset stomach; or homicidal or suicidal thoughts. Think of the revving engine in a car that is in park: it is ready to go when put in drive.

The ***flight*** response involves fleeing or trying to escape the dangerous, threatening, or traumatic event. Someone who responds with flight may have many of these experiences: feeling restless or trapped; shallow, rapid breathing; fidgeting; rapid, darting eye movements; anxiety; or butterflies in their stomach. Think of someone who wants to run away from the situation as fast as they can, faster than their legs will even let them run.

The ***freeze*** response is when a person literally freezes, almost a temporary paralysis, becoming incapable of taking action or moving. Often this is accompanied by feeling cold or numb, chest tightness, difficulty breathing, a sense of dread, or a pounding heart. In this case, the person might want to act but can't. Think of the phrase "deer in the headlights."

The ***faint*** response is almost a dissociative response and a way for the ANS to basically shut down as a defensive mechanism. A person who is experiencing faint attempts to become almost inanimate, as if they do not exist. Think of the phrase "playing possum"—a person who wants to be seen as not alive. A way this response is expressed is in considering *dissociation*: this person is physically present and obviously can't literally disappear but will mentally go to another place in their mind to not be present to the traumatic experience they are enduring. Someone who experiences trauma and responds with faint might blackout during the event as a survival instinct and for self-preservation. This person may never recall the experience, or it may not come to the surface until many years later when the body and brain feel it is safe for the memory to return.

The *fawn* response involves a person filled with a sense of hopelessness and helplessness. This person wants to end the traumatic and/or threatening event and might placate and accept blame or responsibility for the abuse they are incurring to try to please someone or might apologize to avoid conflict and get the situation to stop.

What physical symptoms have you had related to experiences of trauma and adversity? This can be from the examples above or anything else you may have experienced that wasn't included (for example, rapid heartbeat, feeling nauseous or sick to your stomach, clenched fists or jaw, chest tightness, shallow breathing, feeling like you need to go to the bathroom).

_____
_____
_____
_____

What reactions/responses have you had to adversity or trauma, from the examples above or anything else you may have experienced that wasn't included? (For example: yelling, crying, running away, freezing, forgetting, feeling confused or spacey, apologizing, feeling guilty or shameful.) Write them here.

---

something more: when it is helpful and when to flip the switch back

Our physiological and psychological responses, even if uncomfortable or painful, are key to keeping us free from harm. However, F responses (fight, flight, freeze, faint, and fawn) often get activated in situations where they aren't needed or helpful. They may also stay activated in dangerous situations long after the danger is no longer present. Either case can turn into an overactivated nervous system or unhealthy behavior patterns that later lead to a variety of physical and psychological issues. When your body's stress response center is in overdrive or not working properly, it may end up causing you to perceive people or situations as a threat to your safety—often due to past traumas—when, in reality, they may not be dangerous.

Can you think of a time when your reaction to an adverse event or traumatic experience *was* helpful to you in the moment? Write about it here. Describe what happened, how you felt in your body, and how it helped you cope.

_____
_____

Can you think of a time when your reaction *was not* helpful? Write about it here. Describe what happened, how you felt in your body, and how it did *not* help you cope.

_____
_____

Thinking back to that instance, what could you have done differently that may have been more helpful?

Finally, it's important to be able to flip the switch to OFF once the danger has passed. This allows you to regain control (enlisting the help of the parasympathetic "rest, relax, and digest" system described earlier), calm yourself down, and allow your body to recover and rest. By being able to take a step back, reassess, and identify that the traumatic event has passed or the threat is gone, then you can get out of that ANS overdrive state and gently start pressing down on the brakes to get more calm and safe state.

What are some things you have done that have helped you to calm your body after you've been in a dangerous, threatening, or painful situation? List them here.

mindful takeaway

Whenever you feel threatened, your body gives you cues and red flags letting you know that you're in danger or in the presence of a threat. Each of the common responses to stress described here—fight, flight, freeze, faint, fawn—serves a purpose and can help you in the moment to protect yourself in stressful, traumatic, or dangerous situations.

14

identifying your rocks: the things weighing you down

for you to know

People who experience a lot of adversity often have it harder than those who don't. This is a harsh reality! Not acknowledging that someone with adversity has to go through things that others don't would be denying the truth and reality of it.

People with marked AYEs often:
- experience pains and stressors that others don't;
- struggle to get their needs met;
- feel cheated;
- live with a lot of fear;
- find accomplishing their goals and dreams more difficult;
- feel sorry for themselves;
- stay stuck and don't grow or change;
- have a chip on their shoulders;
- have a lot of regrets;
- have resentments toward themselves or others;

- have feelings of shame, blame, and guilt;
- have increased physical and mental health challenges;
- have difficulties with expecting more than people are able to offer; or
- have fewer, and decreased access to, resources.

Think of these things as rocks weighing a person down. Although these rocks aren't physically seen, they impact every aspect of your life—every conversation, thought, action, and decision you make. It's useful to identify these rocks by writing them down. Kept inside, they can fester and grow, making you stuck and even sick.

negative coping behaviors that weigh you down

This example shows what Marie wrote:

Inside the rocks, Marie wrote down her memories of experiences that have had a negative impact on her. These things have been weighing

her down for a long time. Above those memories, she wrote the negative coping behaviors and mechanisms she used. The list that follows includes a short explanation of what these behaviors mean:

- Anger—an intense emotion of wrath or rage after perceiving something was done wrong
- Sadness—despair, gloominess, hopelessness
- Jealousy—resentment toward someone else
- Fear—being afraid of someone or something as threatening or dangerous, feelings of scarcity
- Self-doubt—feeling weak, questioning your abilities, questioning your reality, lacking confidence in yourself
- Self-pity—feeling sorry for yourself or helpless
- Shame—intensely painful feeling of being flawed, not good enough, or unworthy
- Desire—a strong wish or want for something, a strong longing for
- Envy—being jealous of someone, desiring something they have
- Embarrassment—shy, uncomfortable, or guilty feelings in front of others, feeling different than everyone else
- Impatience—being irritable, discontent, restless, or lacking tolerance

- Resentment—feeling regret or a negative emotional reaction to being mistreated you can't have
- Greed—having something but wanting more and more, or wanting something
- Worry—trying to predict an outcome, concern about how you are percieved, focusing your thoughts and feelings on all possible negative outcomes of something
- Feeling sorry for yourself—similar to self-pity, playing the victim, awareness you have less, or are different

This list isn't exhaustive. It follows the rocks from left to right but doesn't include duplicates.

something more: the things weighing you down

Inside the blank rocks, list moments, events, adversities, traumas, and the like that have had a negative impact on you, those things that weigh heavily on you. For example, what are your biggest fears, regrets, and resentments? Fill them in the blank rocks. You can download this illustration at http://www.newharbinger.com/47971.

If Needed, Go to the TiTM Section

Identifying Your Rocks: The Things Weighing You Down

Next, identify the main negative coping behavior(s) for each rock you completed. If you find this hard to do, you can look at the list above for examples. Doing this activity is not meant to cause you pain or lead you to feeling shame, blame, or guilt, but to help you to identify the rocks, those heavy things in your life you're carrying around weighing you down.

> ### mindful takeaway
>
> People can learn to get through the rocks in their life, the things weighing them down, by identifying them. Just because someone used a negative coping behavior before doesn't mean they have to do so moving forward.

15

your relaxation toolkit

for you to know

Sometimes the most productive thing you can do for yourself is relax! Finding things you can do or items you can have with you that make you feel relaxed can "flip your switch" and activate your parasympathetic ("rest and digest") nervous system. You can refer back to Activity 13 as needed. There are countless benefits to the many Rs—rest, relax, recover, reset, reconnect, recalibrate, and recenter—for both your mind and your body. Relaxation techniques and tools can be integral for helping you (1) regain balance when your nervous system is out of whack and needs to be calmed in times of toxic stress and (2) maintain balance when things are already calm.

your relaxation toolkit for mindful moments

What do you turn to when in need of relaxation? What could you put in your relaxation toolkit? Read through this list and circle things you've used to relax, or those that sound appealing to you that you would like to use to have more mindful moments.

    Candles
    Lotion
    Essential oils
    Blankets
    Sweet treats
    Stuffed animals or figurines
    Heating pads
    Music playlist
    Water or hot tea
    Cozy sweater
    Stickers
    Photos
    Books or magazines
    Body pillow
    Keepsakes
    Comfort food
    Headphones
    Flowers and plants
    Go-to movies or TV shows
    Bath bomb or bubble bath
    Board or video game

An Additional TiTM Resource

Add other ideas here:

something more: relaxation activities for mindful downtime

In addition to having items in your relaxation toolkit that help you become or remain calm, you can take this a step further. Think about activities you can do that foster a sense of calm, rest, and relaxation. For a bunch of free mindfulness practices and resources go to https://www.stressedteens.com/toolbox. Here are some ideas:
- Take a warm bath or shower.
- Drink hot tea.
- Listen to a chill or relaxing playlist.
- Watch online or read a self-help video or tutorial.
- Cuddle with a pet.
- Stretch your body or dance around a bit.
- Take some deep breaths.
- Spend time in nature.

- Notice the changes the sun makes throughout the day.
- Look at pictures of nature scenes.
- Pick up a leaf, flower, or pebble from outside.

What activities (either listed here or activities you come up with on your own) can you add to your regular routine to help you feel more relaxed and create mindful downtime? List as many as you want.

_____ _____
_____ _____
_____ _____
_____ _____

mindful takeaway

It is important to keep your mind and body balanced daily by finding mindful moments to just *be*. This is even more important during times of high stress, allowing your body the space to repair and rest. A relaxation toolkit can give you inspiration and ideas for things you can use to create a calm experience for yourself whenever you want or need it.

16

your brain in action: taking in the good

for you to know

Neuroplasticity is the process by which your brain changes in response to experiences. Cutting-edge research in the area of positive neuroplasticity shows that your brain is capable of focusing more on the positive and growing positive neural connections. Essentially you can learn to rewire your brain to create a more positive, happy, hopeful, and joyful life for yourself. It's not easy, but nothing worthwhile or rewarding truly is. Taking in the good is a action to build positive neuroplasticity.

taking in the good

Taking in the good is the process of noticing, attending to, and taking in a beneficial, positive, or pleasant experience as it is occurring—being present for and appreciating what you're doing, even something small and simple. When you engage in healthy activities you enjoy (in moderation: for example, watching your favorite show on Netflix, not going on a two-day Netflix binge and not leaving your room), you get to "take in the good"—you can enjoy them and support your well-being at the same time.

The process can involve something as simple as spending time with someone who lifts you up or makes you feel appreciated, or choosing to listen to one of your favorite songs that inspires you or makes you feel happy. To do this, you first need to be mindful of what's going on in and around you, and then *choose* where to put your attention and time toward. However, taking in the good doesn't have to be overwhelming or take a ton of time: research shows that even spending less than thirty seconds a few times a day looking for the good and taking it in, being present for it, can lead to positive changes in how you feel and your attitude toward yourself, others, and life in general!

something more: where do you want to put your attention?

The action step of mindfulness is to be intentional about where you're putting your attention, awareness, and energy. You can focus on taking in the good—savoring the sweet moments and allowing the positive to get washed through you—rather than only the negative. This requires a bit more hard work since, as you've learned earlier in this book, the human brain is hardwired to go straight to the negative for survival or due to past experiences of adversity and trauma.

To practice training your brain to attend to the positive, complete the following sentences, thinking about recent memories, experiences, and people. Try not to overthink and just write what pops into your mind first:

I felt safe when _____

_____

_____

I felt happy when _____

_____

_____

I felt appreciated when _____

_____

_____

I felt hopeful when _____

_____

_____

I felt confident when _____

_____

_____

I felt relaxed when _____

_____

_____

mindful takeaway

Mindfulness is about paying attention. The next step in developing mindfulness is to be more intentional and thoughtful about where you choose to put your energy and attention, ideally to that which benefits your health and well-being.

17

grounding yourself: calm and connect

for you to know

When you're feeling lost, hopeless, detached, overwhelmed, fearful, or anxious as a result of stress, adversity, or exposure to prolonged trauma of any kind, your nervous system is likely in hyperdrive. This can be draining, exhausting, and can wear you out physically and emotionally. It's important to know some simple, quick ways you can ground yourself to your body and/or the earth and bring yourself back to the present (a go-to list is also provided in Section 1 of this book). Grounding practices like mindful movement can help you engage your parasympathetic nervous system after a stressful situation. Grounding can help reduce pain, lower your cortisol levels (a hormone associated with stress), increase your energy, enhance the speed at which you heal, and bring balance back to your body and mind.

grounding through mindful movement

Part of being mindful is knowing you need to reset and resource yourself, sometimes by engaging in grounding movement. Moving your physical body and connecting to the ground or nature in general is a great way to calm your body when it is overstimulated, bringing you into the present moment if you're experiencing stress, feeling stuck in your head replaying the past, or worrying about what's yet to come. The mindful movement practice introduced here isn't just about walking, but walking is part of it. The goal is to help you get out of autopilot, move through (and ideally, release) your stress, anxiety, or other unpleasant emotions, and connect to your body and the earth.

get outside and ground yourself: mindful movement practice

Find a place outside where you can safely walk around. If possible, find somewhere you can be barefoot (for example, on grass, carpet, or sand) so that you can feel the surface under your feet as you walk. Ideally, this place should have minimal distractions, or at least minimal loud, harsh noises (like cars honking or people yelling). The more relaxing, quiet, and peaceful it is, the better. If this isn't feasible, you can wear headphones or earplugs to drown out some of the noise.

Begin by standing still, noticing the ground beneath your feet. Feel the support it provides. Pay attention to how your feet are positioned, and notice all four corners of your feet and your toes as they press into the ground; notice how the ground presses back into your feet as well, holding you upright. Try to relax your shoulders, jaw, and neck. Let your arms loosely hang at your sides.

Start walking slowly, taking one slow, intentional step at a time, first feeling each heel press down, then the ball of your foot and your toes. Notice how the ground feels as you take each step. Pay attention to the feel of the surface you're on—what texture it is, whether it is warm or cold. For example, if it's grass, feel the blades of grass between your toes.

Next, bring your awareness to the air around you. Notice whether it is warm or cold on your skin, whether there's a breeze or the air is still. Maybe even notice the spaces between your fingers and toes.

Continue walking, feeling the ground beneath your feet and the air around you. As you go, imagine you're literally walking off and moving through your stuck emotions—the trauma, the stress, the anxiety, the anger, the fear—whatever feeling is stuck or trapped inside you that needs to be moved through and out of you. You can picture them passing down through your feet into the earth or out your nose or mouth with your breath as you exhale. If focusing on your breath feels comfortable for you, you could use your breath to help with this. You could imagine breathing in calmness and warmth, safety and support ... then breathing out all the feelings that are no longer serving you and need to be released.

Keep on this way until you feel you have released most of your tension, pain, and stress and have arrived more in the present moment. If you were highly activated before starting this practice, you may still have some residual feelings; that's okay. It's normal to carry some of this with you. It can be challenging to release all of it if you've experienced a severely stressful situation. You could even start again and do this walking practice more than once if desired. Once you feel more grounded, you can stop and congratulate yourself for taking this time to ground yourself in the present.

something more: other grounding techniques to calm and connect

Depending on your environment, resources, personal preferences, and how you're feeling physically and emotionally in the moment, there are many grounding and mindful techniques that can help you reset, get into the present, and recalibrate. ***Grounding focal points*** are physical or functional parts of the body, like the hands or feet, that are always with you. They can be turned toward and noticed at any time and used to bring you into the present.

The list that follows offers other examples of things you can do involving grounding focal points or mindful techniques. Mark any you have tried and found helpful, as well as those you would like to try the next time you could use some grounding.

☐ Find five things you can see, four things you can touch, three things you can hear, two things you can smell, and one thing you can taste.

☐ Hold something in your hand (for example, a rock or a pen) and roll it between your fingers. Think about its texture, weight, and temperature.

☐ Put a rubber band on your wrist and gently pull and snap it, noticing how it feels when it (softly) hits your wrist.

☐ Hold an ice cube in your hand. As it melts, focus on either the point of the most pain/cold, or the places around it where you feel little pain or fewer sensations.

☐ Dig your hands into sand or mud.

☐ Gently press your thumb into your other fingers one at a time.

☐ Put your feet under running cold or hot water.

☐ Splash fresh warm or cool water on your face.

☐ Put your face briefly in the freezer.

An Additional TiTM Resource

☐ Rub lotion into your hands and arms.

☐ Hold a yoga pose, like savasana or downward dog.

☐ Skip outside or do jumping jacks.

☐ Pet an animal.

☐ Jump into or wade in water (a bathtub, shower, lake, river, ocean, or pool).

Add other ideas here:

_____ _____

_____ _____

If you have used any of these techniques when you've felt overwhelmed or been in a state of panic, write about what you did and how it made you feel.

Choose two techniques you would like to do the next time you're in a stressful situation or feel triggered by your adversity or trauma. List them here.

> **mindful takeaway**
>
> Grounding yourself can help you get into the present and calm your nervous system when it's on high alert or overactivated. There are many quick and effective tools you can use to bring yourself back to your body and the earth when you feel overwhelmed or out of control; mindful movement is one of them.

18

choice awareness: the actions you take and the choices you make

for you to know

Past hurts can make it tough to trust our choices or put trust in others. There are so many ways we experience this. Indecision. Uncertainty. Conflict. Hesitation. Vacillation. Lack of clarity. Confusion. Fear of missing out. Fear of rejection. Fear of making a mistake. Facing contradictory choices. Paralysis. Reacting in the heat of the moment instead of thoughtfully responding. Any of these sound familiar or ring true to you?

The shadows from your past, the echoes from the voices of others and of society these often muffle that inner voice speaking the wisdom of your heart and soul. Years of conditioning and messages and adverse experiences may have drowned this intuitive "I" out, making it a distant whisper at times. Intense emotions triggered by past pains can lead to mindless reactions instead of mindful responses. If you've been hurt, if your trust has been violated, if you've made bad choices, how do you know and trust that you're making the *best* and *healthiest* decision for your well-being? And how do you act mindfully rather than react mindlessly? Choice awareness is about zooming in and out and how you see and perceive things. This is part of being mindful—using your awareness to choose where you want to put your attention and focus.

are you HALT?

Awareness of your pain or your fear are often powerful agents for change. The first step in making healthy choices for yourself is checking in and gaining awareness of how you're feeling *before* you make a decision or take a particular action. Check yourself before you disrespect yourself. Often, people react emotionally or impulsively or make choices that don't serve their highest good when they aren't operating on a full tank of gas, are in a lot of pain, or are acting out of fear. Before you make a choice or decide how to respond in a situation, ask yourself these questions using the acronym **HALT**:

Am I **H**ungry?
Am I **A**ngry (or **A**nxious)?
Am I **L**onely?
Am I **T**ired?

If you answered yes to one or more of these, let's work to come up with a solution for how you can first meet your need(s). For example, if you're lonely, you could commit to calling a friend to talk. If you're tired, rest. Table any big choice or decisions until your needs have been met and you're in a better place to make a decision or take action.

something more: choose WISEly

Unfortunately, decisions (both big and small) are often made when you're wrestling with pain, loneliness, emptiness, shame, guilt, blame, conditioning, fears, and self-doubt, and one or more of them wins the battle over your intuitive, knowing self. You're human. It happens. It's totally normal. Just because you made a mistake doesn't make you a failure.

The key is becoming aware, identifying *that* it is happening, *when* it is happening, and owning up to where it is coming from. Then you can make a different choice by becoming **WISE** in your decision-making process.

These four steps can make a world of difference when you start to incorporate them into your daily life choices.

Step 1: **W**ash—Wash away whatever doesn't serve your growth and well-being. In a given situation, whenever possible, ask yourself if choosing to do X thing will help you to grow ... or be good for your physical body, emotional self, spiritual self, relationships, or some other aspect of your life that is of value to you. You might even rate it on a scale of 1–10. Ask yourself where on that scale it falls in terms of how much it contributes to your joy, purpose, health, or growth. If it falls below a 7, say no if you can.

Step 2: **I**ntuition—Listen to yours! You're the only one who is truly able to get you where you want to go. You have the answers inside. No one can tell you how to live your life unless you *let* them. It comes down to you. Make choices that serve you. Trust yourself. Don't cede your power to anyone else. At all times, your gut tells you whether something feels good or not good, right or not right. With all our projections, pains, fears, walls, self-doubts, and judgments, we often choose not to listen to our intuition. One of the best ways to tap into this is to tune into your physical body and go inward. You can do this by closing your eyes, taking a couple of deep, cleansing breaths, and scanning your body to see how you feel. Just notice whatever comes up. Often, great insight will come from this simple practice.

Step 3: **S**urrender—Rather than trying to fight your own thoughts or emotions, or feel the need to prove or justify yourself to others, surrender to yourself. This doesn't mean giving up your power in a dangerous or unsafe situation; this means surrendering to an experience or emotion you're having rather than trying to fight against, prevent, or control it; or to avoid reacting in interactions with others. Let it all go. Just allow whatever arises to be.

Step 4: **E**xcite—As you become more intuitive, more conscious, more aware, more awake, revisit things that used to inspire you and feed your soul. Find new things that excite you as well—who is the new you at a new vibration? You may have different preferences or interests. They may surprise you. Try things out! Be open. What do you like to eat, what music moves you, what movies do you like to watch? It's finally time to ask yourself, truly ask yourself, without judgments or past shadows or echoes interfering: who am I, why am I here, what do I want, and what is going to fuel me every day?

mindful takeaway

You may not have power over certain areas of your life, but you do have power over the choices you make, and you can learn from your past lessons rather than letting the ghosts of your past haunt your present. Learn to respond rather than react by mindfully pausing to assess whether you're HALT—tap into your intuitive self and start making conscious, WISE choices.

19

managing your anger constructively

for you to know

Anger is there for a reason and needs to be acknowledged and named. It brings strength and clarity about your identity and your need to create boundaries. It can be caused by feeling harmed, threatened, or powerless. It ranges in intensity from mild to raging, is expressed in a variety of ways, and is triggered by different things for everyone. Both expressing and suppressing your anger by turning it inward (depression can be described as anger turned inward) can have detrimental effects on your physical and mental health. It is important to learn how to manage and express anger constructively.

constructive ways to manage or express anger

Having strong emotions—for example, anger, fear, or despair—is a healthy, natural thing. The more you try to deny or avoid a feeling, the more it can eat at you over time. No matter what the feeling is, and how unpleasant or undesired it might be, it's there for a reason. We are often told, "Get over it." Ouch. This can feel yucky and invalidating. Instead of the idea of "getting over" feeling a certain way about a painful experience, consider the idea of "getting through" or "moving through" your feelings related to it.

Dr. Peter Levine, who has worked with trauma survivors for decades, says the key to understanding human trauma is what happens during and after the freeze response in animals. Imagine an impala being chased by a cheetah. The second the cheetah pounces on the impala, the impala goes limp. She has "instinctively entered an altered state of consciousness, shared by all mammals when death appears imminent" (Levine and Frederick 1997). It's what the impala does immediately after she escapes that matters. She shakes every part of her body, clearing the traumatic energy that built up. Similarly, neurobiologist Robert Sapolsky writes that zebras and other animals know how to get rid of stress: they simply shake it off and get back to living in the moment (Sapolsky 1994).

It's not so easy for humans to shake it off. If you store pent-up, angry energy inside, it can eat at you and you can end up turning it inward toward yourself, hurting yourself and often resulting in resentment, shame, or depression—or you can end up turning it outward and have an aggressive outburst toward someone else and hurt them. However, there are many ways for us as complex human beings to "shake it off and get through it" like impalas and zebras to clear the energy that has built up.

Here are some constructive ways to release or express anger when it arises, rather than letting it build up.

An Additional TiTM Resource

- Write out all your angry thoughts and feelings. You can even rate your anger on a scale of 1 to 10 before and after you write everything out to see if it changes. You can rip it up and throw it out after if you want.
- Like the impalas and zebras, literally shake your body—either your whole body or just your hands, arms, or legs, or just jump up and down.
- Yell out loud (if it's safe to do so) or silently to yourself in the shower or into a pillow.

- Take ten deep breaths and count as you breathe (breathing in 1, breathing out 1, and so on).
- Do the "destress breath" by breathing in for a count of four and out for a count of six.
- Squeeze your hands together and count to ten.
- Listen to some music—your chill vibes, happy jams, or energy releasers.
- Change your scenery and walk it off, if it is safe and okay to do so.
- Dance it out—pick a high energy song and dance around.
- Change your attention and focus on something or someone that eases you (photos of nature, pets, friends).
- While standing, push your toes and feet hard into the ground.

keep an anger trigger journal

When you find yourself getting heated, you can even keep track of what sets you off and how you respond using a more detailed anger journal. Here are some questions to think about and use as reflection questions to help you be more mindful of your anger:
- What triggered your anger? Consider the people, places, things, and situation.
- Rate your anger on a scale of 1 to 10.

- What thoughts came up?
- What feelings did you notice?
- What physical sensations did you notice in your body?
- What did you do after you became angry?
- How did you feel after the incident?
- How was it resolved?
- Looking back, what, if anything, could you have done differently?

Keeping track of such information can help you gain awareness and insight into what triggers your anger, how to know you're angry, and how you typically respond. You can then learn what is helpful and harmful and how to best handle situations that get you heated and to respond mindfully instead of reacting.

something more: steps to express anger effectively

1. **Mindfully pause.** The first thing to do when you feel yourself getting angry is to take a mindful pause. When you're "seeing red," the parts of your brain that help you with self-control and judgment shut down, so anything you do or say impulsively out of anger is likely to make the situation worse. A pause might involve temporarily removing yourself from the situation or

your environment and taking a minute alone to cool off.

2. **Breathe and count to ten.** Taking time out to notice your breathing, calm down, and assess how you're feeling while you count to ten can give you the space to respond mindfully rather than react mindlessly. You can also enlist any of the suggested actions listed in the previous section of this activity.

3. **Identify the emotions behind your anger.** Often, anger is a mask we wear, and there are other painful emotions behind the anger that trigger it, like hurt, fear, sadness, exhaustion, violation, loneliness, resentment, overwhelm, rejection, or feeling unappreciated or unheard/unseen. Knowing what's behind your anger can be helpful when explaining it to someone else so they understand and possibly empathize more with you. People are more likely to truly listen and hear you if you're able to explain the underlying feeling; for example, saying you felt hurt and rejected instead of just mad.

4. **Use MI-messages.** *MI-messages* (mindful I-messages) are ways to mindfully express your feelings to someone else. They increase the likelihood that whomever

you're talking to will listen rather than becoming defensive and will wait their turn to talk and defend themselves. Steps 1, 2, and 3 involve mindfully checking in with how you're feeling physically and emotionally. Next, you would use this formula to respond to the other person: When you _____ (the behavior), I feel _____ (the feeling) because _____ (the reason). Such statements don't place judgment or blame on the other person (which can be hard if you feel they *are* to blame!) but instead focus on the problem and *your* feelings about it. Since you've already identified your emotions, this is where you can communicate them to the other person. For example: "When you stop by unannounced, I feel violated because I've had boundaries crossed in my past a lot." "When you look at another girl instead of me, I feel rejected because I was ignored a lot in my family." You can write it on paper to acknowledge this for yourself if it isn't safe to tell the person or people how you feel directly.

5. **Be assertive yet respectful, and make a request, not a demand.** Be clear about your feelings, but also be respectful. This could be as simple as saying please or

thanks when requesting what you want from the other person. Requesting rather than demanding makes it more likely that you'll be heard and get your needs met; for example, "I have a request: I'd really appreciate it if you could please look at me while we are talking." This approach comes across much better and will be better received by the listener than "Look at me when I'm talking to you!"

> ### mindful takeaway
>
> Anger is there for a reason and needs to be seen and heard. Once it's been acknowledged, it's helpful to find constructive ways to express your anger that won't hurt yourself or anyone else. MI-messages are one effective way to do this.

Section IV

Pivot and Start Again: Growing Through Adversity

From Surviving to Thriving: Paving the Way Toward Health and Hope

20

setting healthy boundaries

for you to know

Setting boundaries is hard, but important. Learning how to and having the ability to set boundaries is essential to establishing your identity, as well as to having healthy relationships and a balanced life. Unfortunately, this is a skill most of us aren't taught or modeled—and one that can be even more challenging and uncomfortable to learn if you have or are experiencing severe boundary violations, like abuse. It can be scary or make you feel guilty or selfish to assert your boundaries; on the other hand, when your boundaries get crossed, you may feel used, mistreated, violated, resentful, or disrespected. Consider if it is safe for you to enact a boundary.

what are boundaries?

So what exactly are boundaries? **Boundaries** can be physical or emotional limits you set for yourself and range from superflexible to very rigid. Healthy boundaries fall somewhere in the middle of this continuum.

Physical boundaries include your needs or preferences for personal space, your comfort with touch and sexuality, and your physical needs, like rest, food, and water. It's okay to let someone know, if safe, that you need more physical space, that you're not comfortable with being touched or with a certain sexual behavior, or that you're hungry or tired.

Emotional boundaries involve others respecting your feelings and needs (and vice versa); this also includes respecting your *own* feelings and not taking on the responsibility for someone else's. Someone belittling, invalidating, ignoring, or criticizing your feelings are all violations of emotional boundaries.

Safety first! It is important to consider if it is safe to set boundaries in your household or in your romantic relationships. It might not be safe to set these boundaries—if this is the case, please turn to the Resources section at the back of the book. Awareness is the first step to change. If action isn't possible, stay safe first and foremost. At least knowing what your boundaries are or should be, even without action, is an important step. Consider your gut intuition. You can also complete the safety check from Section I to asses if enacting boundaries is safe.

setting healthy boundaries

When you can establish healthy boundaries and you're able to express them to others, you'll likely be doing the following:
- Taking care of yourself
- Asking for what you need
- Knowing who you are, including your values and preferences
- Acting in line with those values and preferences
- Expressing difficult emotions, if safe to do so
- Saying no without explanation or apology
- Saying yes because you want to, not out of guilt or obligation
- Taking responsibility for your own happiness
- Not feeling responsible for others' happiness

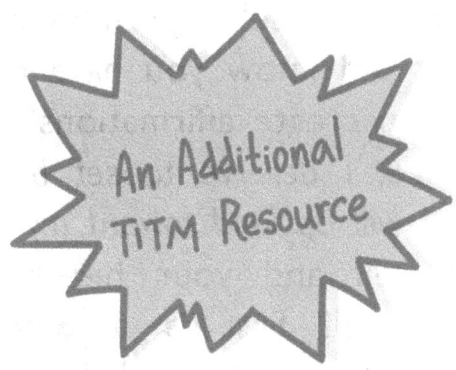

To set healthy boundaries, follow these tips:
- Identify your personal boundaries, both physical and emotional, and your limits.

Consider what you can tolerate and accept and what you cannot. Start to pay attention and develop more awareness of what makes you feel uncomfortable, anxious, or unsafe. You could even write these down somewhere as a reminder to yourself. They're clues about where your boundaries lie and when one is being violated. If you write these boundaries down and it is not safe to keep them, cut up the paper and throw it away afterwards.

- Be kind and compassionate toward yourself. Fear, self-doubt, blame, shame, and guilt are common feelings that arise when you start to enforce boundaries: *Do I deserve to set these boundaries? Am I just being selfish? Will they be hurt or will I be rejected if I do?* These are common questions that may arise out of fear. Give yourself permission to set boundaries and know you have the right to. Perhaps even create affirmations you can tell yourself, like, *I deserve to set boundaries for myself* or *I will be kind toward myself*.
- Make yourself and your health a priority. Putting yourself first is a way of telling yourself that you matter and that your feelings are important; this strengthens your motivation to set and maintain boundaries. By prioritizing yourself, you'll be able to devote more energy and attention to other

key people in your life while also showing up for yourself.
- Communicate what you need *clearly and concisely*. The first step is to figure out what your boundaries and needs are. Once you have a clear idea of these, it's time to clearly communicate these to someone else when they cross a boundary if it is safe to do so. By letting them know in a clear and respectful way, you aren't assuming they are a mind reader. You are also giving them an opportunity to change. Keep it simple and don't overexplain.

something more: no is a complete sentence

It's completely normal to feel the need to explain yourself when you're setting a boundary, but no is an answer and is enough by itself. No further explanation is needed. It's also completely normal to feel bad, strange, or awkward for saying no, especially if you grew up being made to feel bad and were (or are still being) blamed for many things. Learning to say no without explaining yourself is a huge step toward developing healthy boundaries and relationships in your life.

Think of a time when someone asked you to do something that made you feel uncomfortable, anxious, or unsafe—and you did *not* speak up to set a boundary. Describe the situation and what they asked you to do.

_____
_____
_____
_____

How did it make you feel?

_____
_____

What did you do or say in response?

_____
_____
_____

Now think of a time when someone asked you to do something that made you feel uncomfortable, anxious, or unsafe—and you *did* say no and set a boundary. Describe the situation and what they asked you to do.

_____
_____
_____
_____

How did it make you feel?

_____

What did you do or say in response?

_____
_____
_____

> ### mindful takeaway
>
> Setting boundaries and expressing them to others are essential in establishing a healthy sense of identity, healthy relationships, and an overall healthy life. These actions are ways of caring for and respecting yourself.

21

engaging in self-care to be there for yourself

for you to know

Engaging in self-care is not being selfish: it is an act of self-love and essential for your own health and well-being. People often put everyone and everything in their lives before themselves. However, you cannot show up for other people or your daily commitments if you're running on empty. For an example that may hit close to home, consider your cell phone: don't you always make sure to keep it charged so it doesn't run out of juice? If you take such care to keep your cell phone battery alive and well, shouldn't you do the same (if not more!) to keep your own internal battery charged?

Unfortunately, in some environments the only way you are going to get the care and love you need is from yourself. You are deserving of care and love from the important people your life. Sometimes you will need to rely on your own self-care even more. That is why it is even more necessary under these conditions to engage in self-care.

self-care is being there for yourself

Self-care is defined as giving attention to and engaging in ways that support your physical and psychological well-being. How are *you* taking action to preserve or improve your health and well-being? Below are some examples of ways you can take time and do things to be for yourself.

- Spend time with a friend.
- Spend time with an animal.
- Connect with nature/get outside.
- Declutter/organize your space.
- Write in a journal.
- Take a warm bath or shower.

- Play an uplifting song that makes you smile.
- Play relaxing music that soothes your soul.
- Get rest and work on healthy sleep hygiene.
- Maintain healthy limits and use of social media.
- Engage in one of your hobbies or interests.

- Engage in a healthy distraction (like Netflix or YouTube).
- Read uplifting quotes.
- Listen to an inspiring podcast.
- Smile for a few seconds.
- Dance around.
- Take a nap.
- Write down some things that make you feel happy or that you're grateful for.
- Create or make something.
- Cook and eat a healthy meal.
- Move your body; go on a walk.
- Practice one of the grounding techniques described in Activity 17.
- Take a few deep breaths.
- Smell something pleasant.
- Eat something tasty.

    Add other ideas here: _____
    _____

Which of these do you already practice? Which of these would you like to try? Answer these questions in the space below.

using a self-care tracker

We're always encouraged to be there for other people. What about being encouraged to be there for ourselves? To start proving to yourself that you're worthy and deserving of time and care, commit to doing at least one *short-and-sweet* activity that takes up to fifteen minutes per day and one *supersize* activity that takes around an hour per week. Use this self-care tracker to keep a record of these activities. You can download a copy at http://www.newharbinger.com/47971.

Using the self-care tracker below, write down what you did in each category at the end of every day over the next week. You can keep it near your bed and complete it before you go to sleep.

Reminder: Try to get at least one short-and-sweet activity done per day and at least one supersize activity over the entire week. Don't feel obligated to fill in the supersize category daily. If do you get more in, great! It is better to set accomplishable goals and do so in incremental steps.

BE THERE FOR MYSELF: SELF-CARE TRACKER

Day of the week	Short and sweet activity	How did you feel after?	Supersize activity	How did you feel after?
Example: Monday	Listened to one of my happy jam songs	I felt better, less bummed out	Took my dog for a walk	More energetic, happier, focused
Monday				
Tuesday				
Wednesday				
Thursday				
Friday				
Saturday				
Sunday				

something more: a self-care emergency backpack

Self-care is always helpful and necessary. But when you're going through a tough day or a rough period, it's even more critical to take some time out for yourself.

Think about the emergency backpacks many people keep in their car or home in case of a fire or an earthquake. What would you carry around in case of a bad day? These may be many of the same things you listed in the self-care tracker, but there may be other things you rely on when you're having a particularly tough day and need something more.

In the front compartment, you'd put the self-care activities or items that are easy to access, perhaps because they take only a little time or are always available to you with little to no effort. Write down all the easy-access items or activities you want to store in this compartment. These could be some of the same things that fall into the short-and-sweet category, or some different ones you'd rely on more in case of a particularly tough day. Remember to refer back to the list at the start of this activity for ideas.

_____
_____
_____
_____

In the larger compartment, you would put the bigger things you can do to help you with the Rs: rest, reset, refuel, recharge, recalibrate, recover, reconnect. If needed, you can look back at Activity 15. Write down all the self-care activities you want to store here. These could also be some of the same things that fall into the supersize category or others you'd want to turn to specifically on a bad day.

Finally, the hidden compartment inside the backpack would be where you keep all the people and personal keepsakes or momentos you'd want to carry around with you for support. Write down what people or keepsakes (photos, rocks, notes) you'd bring with you in this compartment. It can help to think of who or what you'd turn to when you need to feel safe, supported, loved, reassured, or calm.

mindful takeaway

Self-care is not the same thing as being selfish. It is necessary for your survival and to maintain health and balance. Make a commitment to yourself to *be there* for yourself and engage in some sort of self-care activity every day, even if only for a few minutes.

22

cultivating your gratitude garden

for you to know

More than two decades of research have proven that finding and focusing on the good within us and around us, as well as feeling and expressing a sense of gratitude, are associated with a boost in well-being, happiness, and quality of life and relationships. **Gratitude** is defined as a way of expressing and experiencing appreciation for what you have in your life—emotionally, physically, spiritually, and so forth.

Let's be real though. There are some factors that make it harder, or downright impossible, to get to a place where you feel grateful on a given day. If you've experienced toxic stress, trauma, or adversity, especially early in life, feeling grateful can be even more challenging. However, gratitude has been shown to aid in recovery from loss and trauma by helping people widen their scope to see the big picture and opportunities that can come as a result.

what goes into a gratitude garden

Imagine you have a plot of land and the basic gardening supplies you need to get it going: seeds, tools, plants, fertilizer, and so on. Your land and supplies represent the things you've experienced and the resources you've accumulated up to this point. Think about the trauma and adversities you've endured as affecting the land, specifically the soil in your garden. Your plot of land may be a little or a lot less fertile than, say, someone who had the fortune of never dealing with such experiences. It's probably going to take a considerable amount of time, love, and commitment (TLC) to cultivate and grow a gratitude garden if your baseline is dry soil with no nutrients and limited supplies. And it can be easy, on one hand, to see the dry dirt and the weeds sticking out and, on the other, more difficult to find the beauty and get it healthy and usable again.

Those who haven't had a lot, or any, adversity or trauma in their lives can easily spout off a ton of things they're grateful for, as they look around and see an already beautiful garden. They were set up with a better foundation—more fertile soil with tons of nutrients in it from the get-go. It's likely they were given lots of fertilizer, tools, and seeds, and young flowers, fruits, and vegetables to work with. The playing field definitely started out uneven. If they were asked to draw a picture of their garden and include all the things they're grateful for, it would probably be quite easy.

Just because it may be harder for you doesn't mean you can't find the seeds and budding flowers amidst the dry soil and weeds. It doesn't mean you can't grow a flourishing, beautiful garden teeming with luscious fruit trees, colorful roses, and aromatic herbs. It just might take more effort and focused attention. But couldn't that make it all the more meaningful? Is it possible that there are gifts to these experiences you've endured, like perhaps being a more sensitive and empathic human being? Maybe you are even more grateful because it hasn't just been handed to you; it hasn't been easy to get what so often is just standard or "normal" to someone without such difficulties in their life.

draw your gratitude garden

Ask yourself, "What am I grateful for right now?" In the space on the following page, draw your Gratitude Garden. You can be creative here; there's no right or wrong way to do it. You might write words, quotes, or phrases. You might draw the things, people (or animals), experiences, resources, or abilities that you already have (or have had) that you're grateful for. This could be in the form of flowers, trees, water, or gardening tools. They can be from your past or present.

You can use words or images, or a combination of both.

something more: gratitude in action

Gratitude is more than just thinking about or journaling about the things, experiences, people, places, and resources you're grateful for.

It's also about taking in and appreciating these things *and* putting that appreciation into action. Before you can reap all the benefits, like enhancing your well-being, happiness, and the quality of your life and relationships you have to put some effort into being grateful.

Consider these questions as you take action to express gratitude to yourself and others:

What are some ways to take in and appreciate the things you wrote or drew in your Gratitude Garden? Consider ways to make these things more present in your life— spending time with any of the people you listed, etc.

_____
_____
_____
_____
_____

What are some ways to express your appreciation for the people in your life who've made you feel safe, supported, and loved? Consider telling someone what you are grateful to them for.

_____
_____
_____

What are some ways to express gratitude toward yourself? You can start by saying to yourself, "I am grateful for _____."

In the space below (or on a separate piece of paper), write a letter to someone who was there for you during a difficult time. Tell them what they did for you, how it helped you and made you feel, and what it meant and still means to you.

What you do with this letter is up to you. You can keep it for yourself and enjoy how the experience of writing it made you feel. Or you can show them the actual letter, or read it out loud to them. If you choose to share, the experience can be powerful and deeply meaningful for both of you.

If you've experienced adversity or trauma, being grateful may be harder at times than it is for someone who has the privilege of never having experienced serious loss, pain, or toxic stress in their life. However, the rewards you can reap from cultivating gratitude in your life are profound, and the gifts you can gain from your adversity are many.

mindful takeaway

Don't forget, saying "thank you" to another person or telling yourself "I am grateful for"

_____ is a great beginning to engage in the act of gratitude.

23

your past does not define your future

for you to know

You cannot control what lies behind you—what you've already experienced or endured, the less-than-ideal hand you were dealt in life. True, these things may determine your starting point, and they are *part* of your story. Negative begets more negative, and it is easy to get stuck at the starting line in your *limiting* story of your past—but your opportunity to start over can begin today.

You're more than your past, more than your history, more than your pain, your abuse, your loss, your trauma, your misfortunes. While these things may be part of your story, they don't have to define the present or future you. You don't have to repeat patterns from your own past or your family's. Recent research on post-traumatic growth has found that more than 50 percent of people who endure trauma come out stronger from the experience. Now is your opportunity to begin to focus on what you *want* to create, feel, do, have—and on writing your expansive story of strength and resilience.

coming out the other end: starting a beautiful story of strength

"The most beautiful people I've known are those who have known trials, have known struggles, have known loss, and have found their way out of the depths." This is one of the most poignant quotes from Dr. Elisabeth Kübler-Ross, a woman loved and respected for her major contributions to millions of terminally ill people coping with death and loss in general. She wrote many books on death and dying and came up with the well-known five stages of grief, a model that is still widely used around the world. These stages might not occur in this order. People might be in more than one stage at a time or even think they've completed a stage only to find that, after some time, it comes back.

All of these things are normal and natural—everyone grieves differently. The five stages are:
1. Denial—"No, not me! It can't be true."
2. Anger—"Why me? It's not fair!"
3. Bargaining—Attempting to postpone or stop the pain with "good" behavior
4. Depression—Sadness, hopelessness when reacting to the loss

5. Acceptance—It is happening, or it happened. Now what?

Think about a time when you endured a death or loss. Describe what happened.

_____
_____

Which stages do you remember going through?

_____
_____
_____

Did you ever get to acceptance? If not, how might this have limited you?

_____
_____
_____

Imagine you're talking to a close friend who went through a similar experience, giving them advice and support. What would you tell them to help them see this experience through a different lens? (For example, that it is *part* of their story that makes them who they are but doesn't define them; to view it as beneficial in some way to their growth and resilience; or to help them accept it, integrate it, and to learn to move forward.)

something more: expanding on your story of strength

When she was as young as three and until she was around ten, Maya, now fifteen, was repeatedly told by her stepfather that she was worthless, ugly, and a burden to him and her mother. He often complained that life would be easier without her and said she would never amount to anything. He occasionally threw her against the wall after he had been drinking. Maya has since defined her identity as someone who was abused as a little girl, someone who is worthless and weak, and she still sees ugliness when she looks in the mirror. Maya is terrified of getting close to men, telling herself that all men are unsafe and aggressive. She has defined her present by her past and limited her story in many ways due to these early experiences of abuse.

Think about how much power Maya has given her stepfather. He continues to define her identity and influence the very limiting and negative narrative she has for her life thus far.

Now, briefly consider all the pain, loss, heartache, disappointment, and hurt you've experienced. Reflect on how those experiences have shaped the story you tell yourself. What are the ways you may have been, and may still be, hard on yourself as a result? What self-limiting, judgmental, or self-critical stories do you tell yourself? (For example: *I'm weak. I'm not enough.*)

_____

_____

_____

_____

If you were to write a more expansive, strength-based story, what would you tell yourself instead? (For example: *I am enough. I'm strong. I deserve the best. Not all men are abusive. Some men are kind and compassionate.*) Write that story here.

_____

_____

_____

_____

Actor Keanu Reeves is a perfect example of someone who has endured countless tragedies and thrived despite them all. His father left when he was three; he moved many times throughout his childhood and had to start over with new friends and different schools; his best friend (actor River Phoenix) died of a drug overdose at twenty-three; his daughter was stillborn; and his partner was killed in a car accident. He believes the oft-quoted wisdom that difficulties come not to destroy you, but to help realize your hidden potential.

---

mindful takeaway

Your past is part of your story, but it doesn't have to define you. Your story continues, and in every moment, you have the opportunity to start over and create a more expansive narrative of your life, one of strength and resilience.

24

letting go and forgiving

for you to know

Letting go is never easy. Whether it's a relationship, a belief, an expectation, a pain, or a trauma, it's hard to let go of an attachment or an emotional hold something from your past has had over you. However, letting go and forgiving someone and/or yourself, is actually for your own benefit: it frees you to live a happy and fulfilling life.

letting go for your own well-being

Letting go is for your benefit. It doesn't imply that you have to interact with anyone who hurt you. Letting go can be personal, and it doesn't require involving anyone else. Letting go *is not* the same thing as telling yourself something didn't happen, erasing a trauma or pain from memory, or absolving someone of responsibility for hurting you.

It *is* the personal act of accepting what you cannot change and releasing the control and energy you've let a person or situation have over you. It's about taking your own power back, making space for better things, and choosing somewhere else to invest that energy. It sets you free. It's a way to lighten the emotional or physical hold a person or situation has on you.

We tend to hold our hurts close and relive them again and again. The problem with this is that every time you revisit them, it can bring up the same pain, like picking a scab on an emotional wound that was starting to heal.

Letting go is about freeing yourself of the negative energy you've put into something or someone toxic and what it or they drained from you. It's also about letting go of any fears, resentments, and disappointment over unmet expectations related to the person or whatever it is that happened to you. This is easier said than done, especially if you've been holding on to anger or resentment, you're still grieving unmet expectations, or the person or experience is causing or has caused significant pain or fears to surface. These don't go away overnight; it's okay if it's hard to let go. You've held on for a reason, or often for many reasons. However, when you're able to practice letting go, it frees up more energy, emotions, time, and attention to channel into other healthier places or people.

Think of an experience from your past that brings up negative emotions like anger, resentment, or sadness. Briefly write about it here.

What emotions or feelings come up for you when you think about this experience now?

How does it still have power over you or negatively affect your day-to-day life?

What would be different for you (for example, what you would do, how you might respond to people, how you might feel differently) if you took away the power it has over you and the energy you put into it?

Imagine you wrote the answers to the above questions out on a piece of paper, stuffed it in a bottle, and tossed the bottle out into the ocean to be swept away. Then imagine watching the bottle disappear in the distance. What feelings come up?

What have you made room for in your life and your heart now that you've let go of the hold this experience had over you?

something more: forgiveness as a way forward

Vironika Tugaleva (2017), an award-winning writer and life coach, is someone who knows adversity firsthand as an immigrant and sexual assault survivor. She writes: "The sooner we heal our traumas, the sooner we liberate ourselves from the people who hurt us. By hating them, we hold on to them. We cannot heal."

Letting go is separate from forgiveness; choosing to let go does not directly imply forgiveness. Letting go and forgiving aren't easy, but they're part of the process of healing from past pains so you can move forward and create a better life for yourself. As with letting go, forgiving is *not* the same thing as forgetting. Nor does it mean you're pretending whatever you're forgiving or moving past didn't happen. What's more, forgiving someone else doesn't necessarily mean you have to tell that person—you can do it for yourself, by yourself.

Forgiveness Letter

Consider the people who have hurt you in your life for whom you're still holding on to resentment, a grudge, fear, anger, pain, or disappointment. Write the names of who comes to mind here.

_____

_____

Pick one person from this list who stands out to you for whatever reason. Write their name here.

It can be helpful to release the power, the hold, or the mental energy and effort it takes to carry the pain along with you. Reminder: It is like carrying around a backpack full of rocks—that is the weight of the things you need to let go of and forgive yourself and other for.

In the space below, write a letter to that person forgiving them for what they've done. You could describe what happened, how you felt about it at the time, and how you still feel. At the end of the letter, write a statement or promise to yourself saying that you're choosing to let it go as of today and forgive this other person—and to forgive yourself.

Remember, you don't have to share this letter with them. You're doing this for yourself, to release the power and pain they have had over you and to free yourself. You can also destroy this letter after you write it if you want.

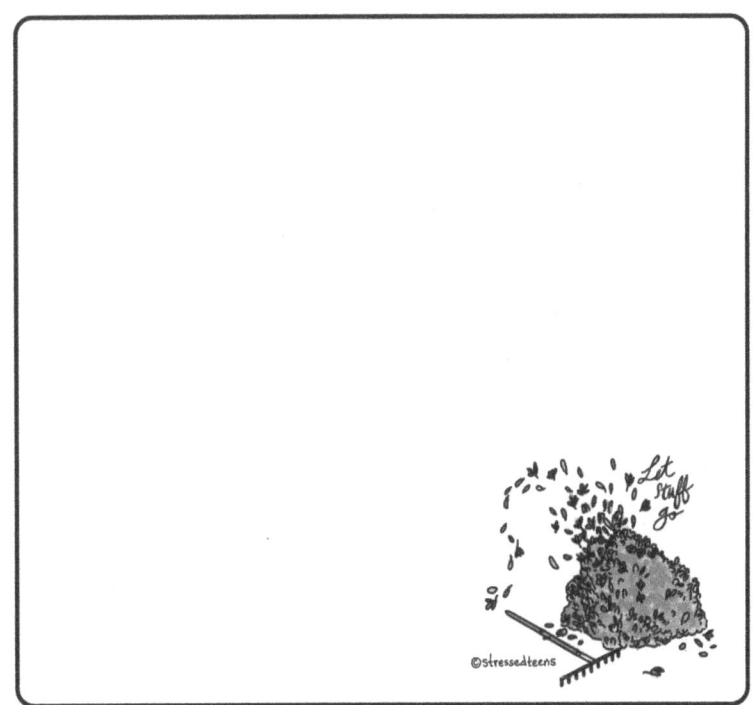

mindful takeaway

Letting go and forgiving are things you do for yourself. They free you and allow you to move forward and release the power something or someone from your past has had over you, and often the related emotions like sadness or anger over unmet expectations.

25

treating yourself with compassion

for you to know

Self-compassion is giving yourself the same kindness you would give to a close friend or pet. We are often our own worst critics, and this tendency can be magnified tenfold if you've experienced a childhood in which you received messages from others that you aren't lovable, worthy of love and respect, or enough as you are. If these messages have become internalized over time, you may now have a cruel roommate living in your head, constantly criticizing or doubting your every thought, feeling, and action. Silencing that inner critic takes practice and time, but it can be drowned out with a voice of self-compassion, kindness, and love.

self-compassion: the antidote to self-criticism

It's likely that you're much harder on yourself than you are on other people. Reflect for a moment on the voice in your head and the things it tells you. Is it often highly critical, judgmental, and just plain mean? Does your inner critic shame you, judge your perceived failures or inadequacies, or point out everything wrong with what you're feeling or thinking, or how you look or act? Would you talk to a close friend the way you talk to yourself? Doubt it!

It's hard to be happy when the closest person to you (yourself) is always being mean and tearing you down. It's even harder to believe positive things about yourself. The first step is having an awareness of that critic and acknowledging your pain. To be compassionate toward yourself, you have to be mindful of your pain and suffering, embrace both the good and the bad, the dark and the light parts of you.

As you've learned throughout this workbook, self-criticism is understandable and normal if, early in life, you were told or felt that you were flawed, unworthy, or undeserving of love or respect. Recent research has even found that people who are compassionate toward themselves are less likely to suffer as much stress, anxiety, or depression from life's challenges than those who are more self-critical. You may carry this belief that self-criticism and judgment are helpful, or even necessary, for self-improvement when, in fact, they actually undermine your ability to thrive. Being compassionate toward yourself is a much more helpful way to learn from your past, become less reactive, boost your happiness, and be more resilient. Your opportunity to rewrite your story begins with an awareness of the presence of that inner critic and then an active, intentional shift toward self-compassion.

Start by asking yourself what it is that you want, and what is healthy, healing, and nourishing for you. Then start telling yourself you're good enough—you're deserving of the things you so deeply desire and need. Forgive yourself for being human; forgive your mistakes and your growing edges. Be gentle with yourself and offer unconditional kindness and warmth. Remember: Recognizing that you might not be getting what you need and deserve in your household does not mean you aren't deserving. What it does mean is that you might need to try and get additional support from others in your life (like from teachers, coaches, friends, and romantic partners).

something more: practicing self-compassion: affirmations

Begin by reading through this list of affirmations a few times. As you read, circle, highlight, or underline the affirmations that stand out or resonate the most with you. These may be the ones you like the most, or the ones you most need to be telling yourself.

I accept myself as I am.
I am enough.
I am worthy of love and respect.
Today, I will treat myself with kindness.
I have strengths and weaknesses, and that's okay.
I can replace fear with strength.
I am releasing myself of self-judgment.
I accept and respect myself, flaws and all.
I make mistakes, and that's okay.
I am doing the best I can.
I am allowed to feel what I feel.
I am worthy of being seen and heard.
I forgive myself.
I don't need others to validate my self-worth.
My struggles and imperfections don't define me.
I am completely lovable just as I am today.
I love myself.

I release patterns that helped me survive but no longer allow me to grow.
I am healing through self-compassion.
I am patient with myself and know I'm doing the best I can.
I am sending love and acceptance to a younger version of me that didn't get it when it was needed.
I am enough! I am me with my gifts and flaws, and for that I am grateful.

Now write your own personal self-compassion affirmations. You can choose some of the affirmations you just read, or you can create your own. Write them here:

You may even want to write these on index cards and keep them with you so you can read them on a regular basis. You could keep them out where you'll see them every day or keep them in a notebook or journal by your bed. They can be loving, friendly reminders to be kind and have compassion for yourself as often as possible.

mindful takeaway

We tend to be our own worst critics, and self-criticism often stems from the voices of others that have become internalized over time. Self-compassion is giving yourself the same kindness you give to others you care about.

26

building your tribe: finding those you can trust

for you to know

It is important, where possible, to choose to spend time with people who lift you up. If you are currently experiencing pain, neglect, abuse, or the like—you probably don't have the luxury of choosing who is around you and how they treat you—and each other. This may leave you feeling powerless and unsafe; however, you have the opportunity to begin to create a "family by choice" of loving and supportive people—your tribe, your positive peeps—who lift you up, encourage you, motivate you, support you, and love you unconditionally! The definition of a tribe being used here is a group of people, or a community with similar values or interests. The sooner you can build your support tribe, the more resilient you will be in the face of adversity.

safe connections are key

Connections are key—but not just any connections: connections that feel *safe*. One of the most well-respected experts on trauma, Bessel van der Kolk (2014), writes about how critical it is to have safe, trusting connections with others: "Being able to feel safe with other people is probably the single most important aspect of mental health; safe connections are fundamental to meaningful and satisfying lives." In disaster-response research, social support is the number one protector against being overwhelmed by stress and trauma. But it's not just the mere fact of *having* social support—it's feeling safe, trusting the other person, being truly seen and heard by them, and feeling you're held in that person's mind and heart. Those are the things that matter. The point of the story is that it's more than just having social support; it's the *quality* of that support.

Even better news: Your tribe doesn't have to be the size of a football team to be meaningful and make a difference; it can consist of only one person. One safe and trusting relationship can make all the difference. Quality over quantity. But building a tribal community that extends beyond one key support person is the icing on the cake here.

the science behind the need to feel safe

For your body to calm down after you've felt threatened or experienced a trauma of some kind, you need to feel like you're safe. Trauma triggers changes in the signals you receive in your **ventral vagal complex** (VVC), the part of your brain that tells you that you're now safe. As your system begins to downregulate, the VVC sends signals to slow down your breathing and your heart rate to make you feel calm, relaxed, and centered. If you're in danger or traumatized, your ultimate emergency system in the brain is activated. As you go into freeze, fight, flee, faint, or fawn (the 5 Fs from Activity 13) there are a number of ways your body may react—your heart rate dropping, your metabolism slowing down, and your gut emptying are just a few examples.

The more your brain experiences feelings of safety, trust, and connection in relationship to others, the more you can both grow *and* repair the VVC, that part of your brain that makes you feel safe, calm, connected, and engaged. So what does this mean? Those who have had experiences where their safety and trust were violated can have different types of relationships later on. This can also be accomplished with our furry companions! Dogs, horses, and dolphins are used to provide a sense of companionship for people experiencing trauma who have trouble relating to other humans. The key here is the need to recover experiences of safety, reciprocity, and relaxation. Although you might not be able to swim with the dolphins right now, it is important to work toward getting your needs and wants met.

Think of one person or animal with whom you feel (or have felt) a sense of safety and calmness. Who is it and what are/were they like?

_____

_____

What have they said or done specifically that makes/made you feel safe and calm?

_____

_____

something more: building your tribe

Now go beyond the one person (or animal) you just wrote about, and reflect on your whole life. Think of all the people (and possibly animals) throughout the various stages and places you've been who have made, or make you feel good enough, safe, secure, trusting, calm, nourished, seen, heard, appreciated, and understood. In the space below, draw a representation of your tribe: who is in it and what it looks like. There's no right or wrong way to do so. Whatever images, symbols, shapes, and words come up are all valid and important parts of the tribe you're building and want to hold close.

Nurturing Relationships with Your Tribe

Once you've begun building your tribe, at least in your head, and come up with who and what beings are included, it's time to take action to nurture your relationships. Putting this into action could include:
- Taking the time to tell someone you appreciate something they did for you or something kind they said to you.
- Scheduling quality time with one or more of them, perhaps organizing an activity you both enjoy and could do together.

- Communicating to someone what they mean to you, or share something you admire or value in them (for example, about how they have handled difficulties in their own life).
- Doing something thoughtful with the other person's interests in mind (for example, if your friend loves animals, you could surprise them and take them to an animal shelter to volunteer; if this person is into trying different kinds of foods, plan a night where you cook a new dish.

The idea here is doing things that require intention, effort, and to communicate to your people *I see you, I hear you,* and *I appreciate you.* Research shows that people are happier when doing good for others. Moreover, it can bring you closer to people you care about when this good is directed toward them, or vice versa.

What are some actions you can take to nurture your relationships? Write some ideas here.

mindful takeaway

Social support is key to dealing with and overcoming adversity in your life. Specifically, having safe, trusting connections can lead to more resilience and better health. Who is in your tribe?

27

one day at a time: drop your rocks to lighten your load

for you to know

You can live your life one day at a time. You can start your day over anytime you want. You don't have to wait for tomorrow to start anew. Every moment is a new opportunity to start fresh and do something different. Just because you did something one way before doesn't mean you have to do it again. Also, you don't have to think about forever or the rest of your life, but just right now. Change takes time, but by taking action and making incremental changes, you'll see how things can shift and change for you.

positive coping skills: healthy ways of managing adversity

In Activity 14, you learned about healthy and safe coping skills (aka positive coping skills): those positive mental reminders, strategies, or actions you can take to help support your mood, ease your stress, and manage your problems. In this activity, you'll be focusing on some of the positive coping skills you have or can use.

As you can see in this illustration, Marie has made changes in how she deals with the rocks in her life. The things inside the rocks, those things weighing Marie down, haven't changed and can't be changed, but how she chooses to manage them has changed. She's crossed out the negative coping behaviors, those unhealthy ways of thinking and behaving, and has now listed those positive coping skills she's working to use instead. It doesn't mean that she's perfect at this, but she's working to replace those negative ways of behaving and thinking with more positive, healthy, and safe skills that are more beneficial to her health and well-being. With these changes, the impact on her life and functioning has shifted a great deal to the positive.

Look at the new ways Marie is dealing with her rocks. This list of positive coping skills offers short explanations of what they mean, or how they may look in someone's life.

- Self-respect—pride, confidence, and a belief in yourself
- Patience—being able to accept or tolerate a delay or that things might not be the way you want (or need) them to be
- Self-acceptance—accepting and loving yourself as you are right now
- Forgiveness toward another (not necessarily with the person or people involved)—to stop feeling resentment against someone who did

you wrong, to lessen the intensity and weight it is putting on you
- Courage—bravery to do something hard, even if it goes again the grain, to do what is right for you
- Take action—engaging in incremental steps to manage or resolve the problem or issue; working to change where it is possible and safe to do so
- Gratitude—a way of expressing and experiencing appreciation for what you have or who you are, or toward another person or pet
- Tolerance—a fair and open attitude toward opinions and actions different from your own; to be with situations or people you can't necessarily change, adjusting your expectations of what is possible of yourself or others
- Safety—protection, security, feeling not threatened
- Self-preservation—taking the needed steps to protect yourself from harm whenever and wherever possible
- Grieve—suffering grief or mourning a loss
- Self-love—loving and appreciating yourself, feeling worthy
- Act of generosity—doing something kind for the sake of doing it

- Self-forgiveness—forgiving yourself; forgiveness is a process that is possible
- Letting go—the act of accepting what you cannot change; to lessen the intensity or hold something has on you, mentally or physically
- Acceptance—accepting another not necessarily with the person (or people) involved; accepting the things you can't change

This list isn't exhaustive. It follows Marie's rocks from left to right but doesn't include duplicates.

something more: lighten your load

Refer back to the rocks you identified in Activity 14, then read these instructions through before continuing.

First, copy the content from *inside* the rocks on this new image; you can also download a copy at http://www.newharbinger.com/47971. If there is something that is not a rock for you right now, you don't need to include it. Also, if there is something new, you can consider adding it.

Now, for each rock:
- If you're still engaging in the negative coping behavior(s), just write the same one(s) in the rock in upper-case letters.
- If you have reduced using the negative coping behavior(s), even a little bit, write it in the rock in lower-case letters.

- If you can see where you could replace one or more of these negative coping behaviors with a positive coping skill, draw a line through the negative coping behavior like Marie did, and list the positive skill(s) in the rock.

As you move forward, use as many of the positive coping skills you've listed as you can. This is about progress, not perfection. Work to line through or even erase the negative coping behaviors to end up with as many positive coping skills as you can.

mindful takeaway

Lighten the load of the things weighing you down by using positive coping skills to manage the adversities in your life.

28

the bank of well-being

for you to know

As described in Activity 16, taking in the good is about seeking out and engaging in healthy things to do and/or noticing the things you're already doing that can benefit you in some way. Once you engage in something that is positive, pleasant, or beneficial in some way, you can take it in by noticing, and attending to it—almost as if you're savoring the sweetness of it. You're taking in the benefit or good the experience has to offer. Taking in the good allows you to enjoy things as they're occurring, making them part of your experience in the moment.

You're also creating a lasting resource for your "well-being bank." Think of taking in the good as one of many "coins" that you can add to your virtual savings account. You can use these saved coins to draw upon, especially in tough times when you need support the most.

the bank of well-being

Think about real-life emergencies. When people need money in an emergency, they often go to the bank and get money they've saved. If someone doesn't have the money they need, it's difficult to deal with the emergency. Similarly, when you're dealing with a difficult time in your life (whether stress, a health problem, adversity, trauma, or the like) it's hard, if not impossible, to manage when you have no savings, or resources, to pull from.

When you're being mindful, practicing gratitude, and grounding yourself, for example, you're adding more coins to your bank. These coins get stored and act as resources you can pull from to help you be better able to tolerate and manage whatever difficulties life throws your way. The more coins you put in your bank of well-being, the more resources you have saved to call on in times of stress or hardship. These are the times when you can take advantage of all the tools and resources available to you. In this bank of well-being, you'll see examples of coins, or resources, that can contribute to your well-being.

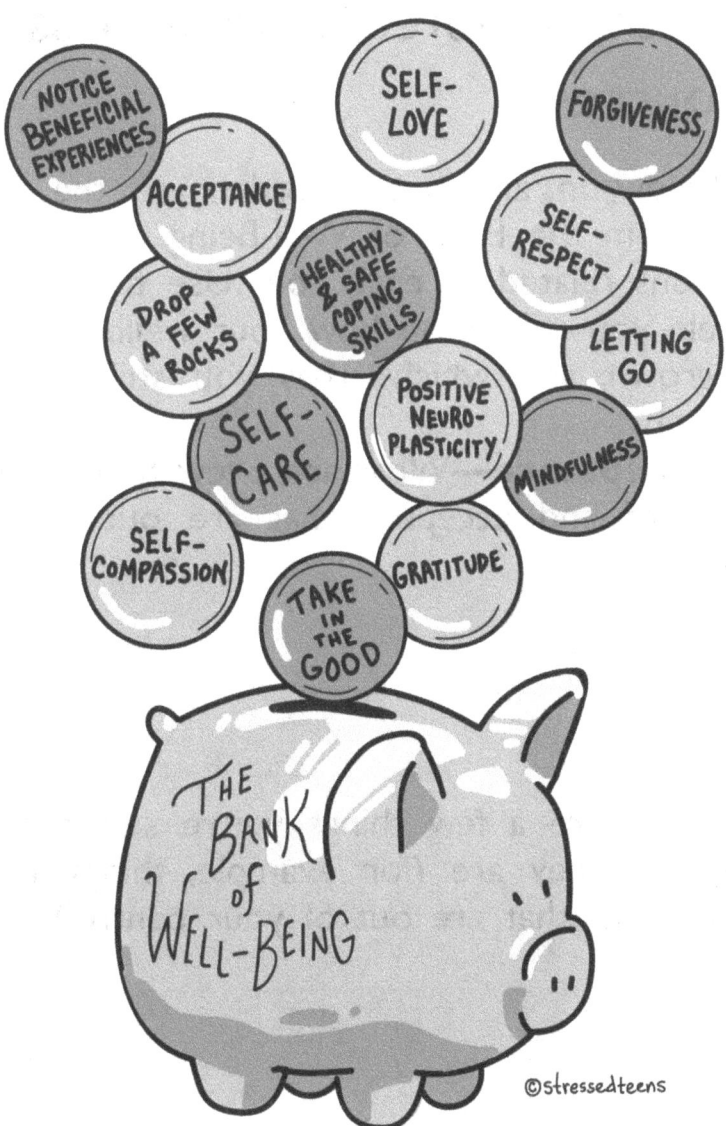

something more: the value of saved resources

Below, in alphabetical order, are the coins listed from the Bank of Well-Being. Answer the questions related to each coin. Use the answers to help you reflect on how your wellbeing bank has grown, and which areas you still want to work on.

Acceptance—What are a few things you've let go of and accepted that are out of your control?

_____
_____
_____

What are a few things you're struggling to accept as they are (for example, things you're upset about that are out of your control)?

_____
_____
_____

Drop a few rocks—What are a few of the negative coping behaviors you've changed or use less?

_____
_____
_____

What are a few positive coping skills you've brought into your life or use more?

_____

_____

Forgiveness—Have you started to forgive yourself when you need forgiving? Have you started to forgive others in your life, if you need to forgive them to move forward for yourself? What does forgiveness mean to you?

_____

_____

_____

Gratitude—Do you consider what you're grateful for each day, big or small? Thinking about what you're grateful for can shift your mood in the moment. Write down three things you're grateful for right now.

_____

_____

_____

Did it change your mood even a little?

_____

Healthy and safe coping skills—What are five healthy and safe coping skills you're using? (Refer back to those skills you picked in Activity 7).

1. _____
2. _____
3. _____
4. _____
5. _____

Letting go—What is something that you're now able to let go of, or are working on letting go of, to free up energy and space you can invest in healthier places, people, and activities?

_____
_____
_____

Mindfulness—What are two things you think of when you think about mindfulness and how are you using it in your life? (Refer back to Activity 12 for help).

_____
_____
_____

Notice beneficial experiences—What experience has benefited you in some way since you woke up today (for example, the weather being nice enough that you don't need a sweater, or remembering to bring your glasses to class)?

_____
_____
_____

Positive neuroplasticity—What are three things you can do more of to train your brain to tilt toward the positive (for examples, a positive activity, feeling a positive emotion, spending time with people who build you up)?

_____
_____
_____

Self-care—What are two self-care activities you're engaging in or can engage in on a regular basis?

_____
_____

Self-compassion—What are two affirmations you can tell yourself right now that express compassion toward yourself? (See Activity 25).

_____
_____

Self-love—What are three things you do, or can start to do, to show yourself that you love yourself?

_____
_____

Self-respect—How do you show yourself respect (or if you don't, how can you start doing so)?

_____
_____

Take in the good—How will you take in the good and support your well-being? Write down two specific things you can do at least once a week.

_____
_____

> ### mindful takeaway
> The more things you can do to create positive, healthy resources for yourself, the more "coins" you can add to your "bank," and the more you'll enhance your overall health and well-being.

29

resourcing yourself

for you to know

This book in its entirety is about providing you with awareness and insight to empower you with a myriad of skills, tools, and resources to help you create a well-being savings account. Your well-being bank is now full of resources to turn to when you're having a mental health emergency. You've also learned many skills to keep and stay safe if in a safety emergency (for example, those listed on the protective porcupine).

resourcing yourself

Resourcing yourself is the process of using healthy and safe coping skills, and engaging in self-care activities and related tools that benefit your health, wellness, and well-being. Using healthy and safe coping skills, like those from the list of one hundred, or those you wrote on your top ten list, is beneficial to you in the moment. However, the secondary benefit is also powerful and long-lasting: it involves all the "resources" you get later. When you do things that are beneficial to you, you can turn to these resources to help you when life is hard. If you've been doing things that are to your benefit on a regular basis, the harder things are, the easier they'll be to tolerate.

something more: your well-being bank

Using the image you can download at http://www.newharbinger.com/47971 or the one here, list all the coins you can think of that you have in your bank of well-being and can continue to use. You can look back at the version in Activity 28 for ideas.

Here are some topics in the book to consider:
- Self-care activities from the "Be There for Yourself: Self-Care Tracker"
- Your top ten healthy and safe coping skills
- Rocks you've dropped that have lightened your load
- Things you've have let go of that are out of your control
- The TITM that resonated with you most throughout this book

mindful takeaway

The more you resource yourself, the more coins you will have in your bank of wellbeing and the more supported you'll feel during times of stress, adversity, and trauma.

30

controlling the controllables

for you to know

Like others who experience stress, adversity, and trauma, you may have ongoing difficulties related to fear and acceptance.

What we mean here is the mental side of fear; for example, fear of how something will turn out or how something went, fear about what others think, fear about what other people will or won't do, or fear that you won't have something you need (for example, money or safety).

And by acceptance, we mean accepting things in and out of your control. You may find yourself wanting to control how something will go. However, if those things involve other people, or are things you don't have the power to change, they're out of your personal control.

controlling the controllables

Learning how to take charge of the areas of your life that are in your control is useful. Why fear the things you can't change? Why try to get people to change when you can't control them? As much as you may want it to be otherwise, the only person you can change is yourself. You can make suggestions for someone to change. You can make plans to effect change where you can, but the rest is out of your control.

You can make changes, take action, and create needed plans in areas you can control. In areas you can't control, your work is to stop trying to control them. For example, you don't have the power to control other people or things in larger society, like a global pandemic.

Differentiating between those things that are in and out of your control can greatly help you get a handle on things in your life, decrease unneeded fear, and accept more of what you can and can't change.

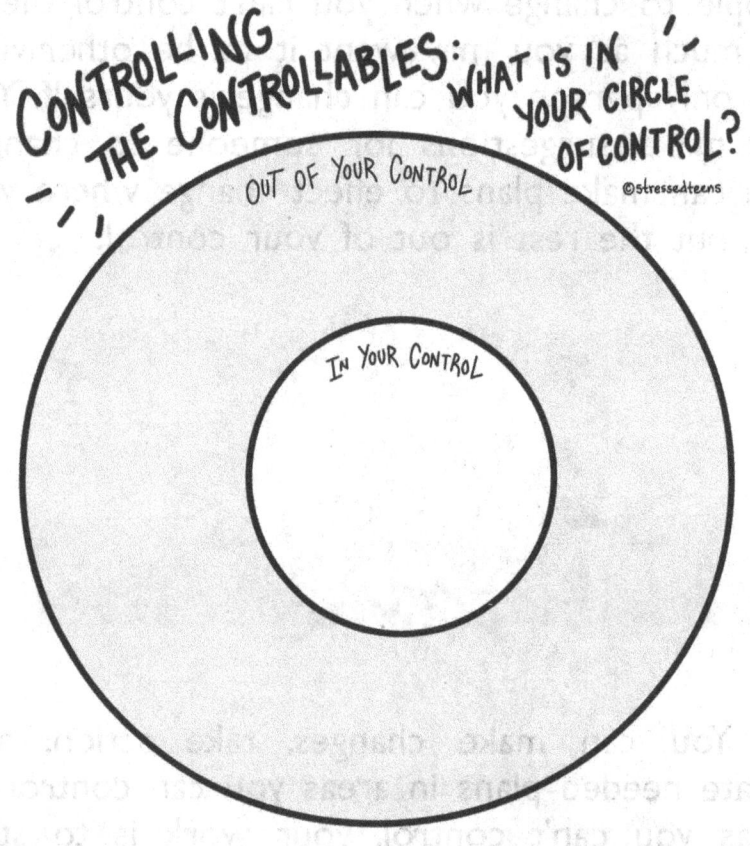

Look at the previous illustration, and ask yourself, *What is in my circle of control?* Take some time to reflect on your answer. Think about things that have come up for you in this book that you still find bothersome. Use the following as areas to dive a bit deeper:
- Areas of your life that you have continued pain and suffering over
- Adversities you're experiencing that affect your safety (emotional and/or physical) or security

- Familial, peer, and romantic relationship concerns and difficulties with feeling at peace and contented
- Areas in your life where you feel stuck or can't seem to let go
- People or things that cause you a great deal of fear and uncertainty

Using this list as a prompt, complete *Controlling the Controllables* by listing those things in and out of your circle of control; you can download a copy at http://www.newharbinger.com/47971. When something bothers you, first ask yourself, *Is this in or out of my control?* If it is in your control, what can you do about it? If it is out of your control, what parts can you change that keep your interest at heart?

Work on letting go of those things you can't control. Work to accept what you can and can't change. Consider taking action and making plans to change something you sit in fear of. Throughout this book, we have been offering you skills to learn and continue to use over the course of your life. We wish we had learned these skills when we were younger:

- How to make changes in controlling what you can affect change over
- How to adjust your expectations
- How to bring more acceptance into your life
- How to lessen some of the fear you have

All of these are useful beyond measure! Since we need to close this book, we want to leave you with as many practical skills as possible, so when life shows up, because it will, you know what to do, or at least know where to turn in this book as a guide to help you navigate the situation.

something more: moving forward one day at a time

You aren't going to change 180 degrees after completing this book. What you've begun is the process of becoming more aware of and knowledgeable about your life, and understanding that change and growth can unfold if you're open to them. Remember, you aren't defined by the adversity and trauma you've endured. You aren't the things that happened to you—you're who you define yourself to be. You determine your future by the choices you make and the actions you take. Be gentle with yourself, remember that change takes time, take incremental steps toward change, advocate for yourself where possible, and remember that self-love, compassion, and care are necessary antidotes to pain and suffering.

As you close this book, take a few minutes to reflect on your life right now. If you were to reread it in three or six months, what would you want to tell yourself? What would you want to remember as the most important takeaways and/or "aha moments" you've had during this journey of self-discovery? Write these in the space provided.

For Inquiry, Awareness, and Insight

Now, set a reminder in your calendar or make a note to come back in three months, and maybe again in six months, to read what you've written. Reflect on your continued growth and change, and consider any areas where you're still stuck or struggling and could use some refreshing from the parts of this book that were the most meaningful to you.

> ### mindful takeaway
>
> No one will value you more than you're willing to value yourself. You're worthy. You're lovable. You matter. If anyone tells you otherwise, they probably don't have your best interest at heart. Work on letting go of those things you can't control. Work to accept what you can and can't change.

Safety Check

SAFETY CHECK

Here are the steps to do a safety check:

1. Who are you with? _____ Are you safe? _____
2. What are you doing? _____
3. What are you thinking? _____

4. Where are you? _____ Are you safe? _____
5. Why are you in this situation? **Not** for self-blame, shame, or guilt, but if possible, not to put yourself in the same situation again. The why is the context of the circumstances that got you to the current situation.
_____
_____

6. How are you feeling physically? Describe what you are feeling in your body.
_____
_____

7. How are you feeling emotionally? Describe these feelings.
_____
_____

@stressedteens

I Need Immediate Assistance Right Now

If you're engaging in self-harming behaviors, please consider telling someone you can trust: a school counselor, a family member, a friend. If you're in immediate danger, call 911!

Emergency Contacts

These resources can provide additional assistance and information.

National Suicide Hotlines: 1-800-SUICIDE (784-2433) or the 988 Suicide and Crisis Lifeline: 988 or 1-800-273-TALK (8255)

Both are toll-free, 24-hour, confidential hotlines that connect you to a trained counselor at the nearest suicide crisis center.

988 Suicide and Crisis Lifeline: https://988lifeline.org

This website offers details about how to call if you need help, how to identify suicide warning signs, and information for many different groups experiencing mental distress.

International Suicide Hotlines: http://www.suicide.org/international-suicide-hotlines.html

Crisis Text Line: https://www.crisistextline.org or text HOME to 741741

Teen Central, a free and safe prevention and intervention resource: https://teencentral.com

National Runaway Safeline: https://www.1800runaway.org or call 1-800-RUNAWAY

Mental Health Resources and Community Resources Specific to Victims of Violence and Social Disadvantage

General Mental Health

Stressed Teens: Visit https://www.stressedteens.com

To contact the authors of this book, please email training@stressedteens.com

National Hopeline Network, Suicide and Crisis Hotline: 1-800-784-2433

Teen Line: Visit https://teenlineonline.org, call 1-800-852-8336, or text TEEN to 839863

National Alliance on Mental Illness (NAMI): Visit www.nami.org or call 1-800-950-6264

Society for Adolescent Health and Medicine (SAHM): Visit https://www.adolescenthealth.org/Home.aspx

Post-traumatic Stress Disorder (PTSD)

Mayo Clinic: Visit https://www.mayoclinic.org/diseases-conditions/post-traumatic-stress-disorder/symptoms-causes/syc-20355967

PTSD Alliance: Visit http://www.ptsdalliance.org/help/

NAMI: Visit https://www.nami.org/About-Mental-Illness/Mental-Health-Conditions/Posttraumatic-Stress-Disorder

Anxiety and Depression

Anxiety & Depression Association of America (ADAA): Visit https://adaa.org

Erica's Lighthouse: A Beacon of Hope for Adolescent Depression: Visit www.erikaslighthouse.org

Substance Use and Abuse

Substance Abuse and Mental Health Services Administration (SAMHSA): Visit https://www.samhsa.gov/find-help/national-helpline or call 1-800-662-4357

Eating Disorders

National Eating Disorders Association: Visit www.nationaleatingdisorders.org or call 1-800-931-2237

Bullying

Teens Against Bullying: Visit www.pacerteensagainstbullying.org

Cyberbullying Research Center: Visit https://cyberbullying.org/resources

Issues Related to Gender and Sexual Identity

LGBTQ Resources: Visit www.glaad.org/youth or www.gsanetwork.org

LSEN (an organization that focuses on LGBTQ issues in education): Visit www.glsen.org

Trans Lifeline: Visit https://translifeline.org or call 1-877-565-8860

Victim of Abuse/Domestic Violence/Intimate Partner Violence/Victim of Crime/Trafficking

National Dating Abuse Helpline (Love Is Respect): Visit www.loveisrespect.org, text LOVEIS to 22522, or call 1-866-331-9474

Safe Place: Visit https://www.nationalsafeplace.org or text 44357

Tribal Resource Tool (Resources for Survivors of Crime and Abuse): Visit https://tribalresourcetool.org

National LGBTQ Institute on Intimate Partner Violence (IPV): Visit https://lgbtqipv.org

National Center for Victims of Crime (NCVC): Visit https://victimsofcrime.org

Gender-based violence and related issues: VAWnet: Visit https://vawnet.org

STAND! For Families Free of Violence: Visit https://www.standffov.org or call 1-888-215-5555

Polaris (Human Trafficking): Call 1-888-373-7888, text HELP to 233733, or visit https://polarisproject.org/human-trafficking or https://humantraffickinghotline.org

National Child Abuse Hotline/Childhelp: Visit https://www.childhelp.org or call 1-800-422-4453

National Sexual Assault Hotline: Visit https://www.rainn.org or call 1-800-656-4673

California Victims Resource Center: Visit https://1800victims.org or call 1-800-842-8467

Other Resources

National Coalition for the Homeless: Visit https://nationalhomeless.org

Safe Housing Partnerships: Visit https://www.safehousingpartnerships.org

Legal Assistance: Visit https://teenlineonline.org/youth-yellow-pages/legal-assistance or https://www.hbcfl.org

National Network for Immigrant and Refugee Rights (NNIRR): Visit https://nnirr.org

For Inquiry, Awareness, and Insight

References

Felitti, V.J., R.F. Anda, D. Nordenberg, D.F. Williamson, A.M. Spitz, V. Edwards, and J.S. Marks. 1998. "Relationship of Childhood Abuse and Household Dysfunction to Many of the Leading Causes of Death in Adults: The Adverse Childhood Experiences (ACE) Study." *American Journal of Preventive Medicine* 14(4): 245–258.

Kübler-Ross, E., and D. Kessler. 2014. *On Grief and Grieving.* Commemorative ed. New York: Simon & Schuster.

Levine, P.A. and A. Frederick. 1997. *Waking the Tiger: Healing Trauma.* Berkeley, CA: North Atlantic Books.

Porges, S.W., and D. Dana. 2018. Clinical Applications of the Polyvagal Theory: The Emergence of Polyvagal-Informed Therapies. New York: W.W. Norton & Company.

Sapolsky, R.M. 1994. *Why Zebras Don't Get Ulcers: A Guide to Stress, Stress-Related Diseases, and Coping.* New York: W.H. Freeman.

Tugaleva, V. 2017. *The Art of Talking to Yourself.* Soulux Press.

Van der Kolk, B. 2014. *The Body Keeps the Score: Brain, Mind and Body in the Healing of Trauma.* New York: Penguin Books.

Yerkes, R.M., and J.D. Dodson. 1908. "The Relation of Strength of Stimulus to Rapidity of Habit-Formation." *Journal of Comparative Neurology and Psychology* 18(5): 459–482.

Gina M. Biegel, MA, LMFT, is a California-based psychotherapist, researcher, speaker, and author who specializes in mindfulness-based work with adolescents. She is founder of Stressed Teens, which has been offering mindfulness-based stress reduction for teens (MBSR-T) to adolescents, families, schools, professionals, and the community since 2004. She created MBSR-T to help teens in a large HMO's outpatient department of child and adolescent psychiatry whose physical and psychological symptoms were not responding satisfactorily to a multitude of other evidence-based practices.

Biegel is an expert and pioneer of bringing mindfulness-based approaches to youth. She is author or coauthor of the *The Trauma and Adversity Workbook for Teens, Take in the Good, The Stress Reduction Card Deck for Teens, The Mindfulness Workbook for Teen Self-Harm, Be Mindful and Stress Less, Mindfulness for Student Athletes, The Stress Reduction Workbook for Teens,* and *Be Mindful.* She also has a mindfulness practice audio CD, *Mindfulness for Teens,* to complement the MBSR-T program. She provides worldwide multiday trainings and intensive ten-week online trainings, and works with teens and families individually and in groups. Her work has been featured on *The Today Show,* CNN, *Psychology Today, Reuters, The New York Times, US News & World Report,* and *Tricycle* to name a few. For more information, visit her website at www.stressedteens.com.

Stacie Cooper, PsyD, is a published author, transition coach, and Pilates and mindfulness instructor with twenty years of experience helping teens and young adults on their journey to uncover their strengths, find purpose, and navigate major life transitions. In 2009, she graduated from Pepperdine University with her doctorate in clinical psychology, and completed her training at Duke University's student counseling center.

Stacie has had a passion for working with youth in transition and women for her entire career, and founded Aware and Thriving in 2016 to focus on preventative and strengths-based efforts emphasizing mind and body. She has been a mentor for Girls Incorporated's College Bound Mentorship Program, and a keynote speaker for their Eureka summer camp for middle school girls. She teaches group reformer Pilates classes in the local community, and private reformer sessions out of her house. See www.awareandthriving.com for more information.

Illustrator **Breanna Chambers** specializes in watercolor, ink, and digital mediums. She is the illustrator for *Take in the Good*. She currently lives in San Luis Obispo, CA, with her partner and her cat, Mr. Goose.

Foreword writer **Rhonda V. Magee** is a renowned mindfulness teacher and innovator of mindfulness-based social justice principles, concepts, and practices. She is professor of law at the University of San Francisco.

More Instant Help Books for Teens
An Imprint of New Harbinger Publications

OVERCOMING SUICIDAL THOUGHTS FOR TEENS
CBT Activities to Reduce Pain, Increase Hope, and Build Meaningful Connections

THE ANXIETY AND DEPRESSION WORKBOOK FOR TEENS
Simple CBT Skills to Help You Deal with Anxiety, Worry, and Sadness

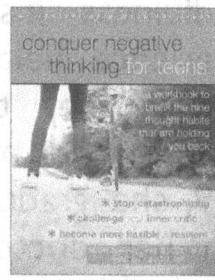

CONQUER NEGATIVE THINKING FOR TEENS
A Workbook to Break the Nine Thought Habits That Are Holding You Back

THE RESILIENCE WORKBOOK FOR TEENS
Activities to Help You Gain Confidence, Manage Stress, and Cultivate a Growth Mindset

THE RACIAL TRAUMA HANDBOOK FOR TEENS
CBT Skills to Heal from the Personal and Intergenerational Trauma of Racism

THE GROWTH MINDSET WORKBOOK FOR TEENS
Say Yes to Challenges, Deal with Difficult Emotions, and Reach Your Full Potential

newharbingerpublications
1-800-748-6273 / newharbinger.com
(VISA, MC, AMEX / prices subject to change without notice)
Follow Us

Don't miss out on new books from New Harbinger.
Subscribe to our email list at **newharbinger.com/subscribe**

Did you know there are **free tools** you can download for this book?

Free tools are things like **worksheets**, **guided meditation exercises**, and **more** that will help you get the most out of your book.

You can download free tools for this book—whether you bought or borrowed it, in any format, from any source—from the New Harbinger website. All you need is a NewHarbinger.com account. Just use the URL provided in this book to view the free tools that are available for it. Then, click on the "download" button for the free tool you want, and follow the prompts that appear to log in to your NewHarbinger.com account and download the material.

You can also save the free tools for this book to your **Free Tools Library** so you can access them again anytime, just by logging in to your account! Just look for this button on the book's free tools page.

+ Save this to my free tools library

If you need help accessing or downloading free tools, visit **newharbinger.com/faq** or contact us at **customerservice@newharbinger.com**.

Back Cover Material

your go-to toolbox for healing trauma & building resilience

Do you often feel emotional, moody, anxious, angry, or upset? Do you no longer enjoy the things you used to, or feel overwhelmed like the world is just too much? If you've experienced extreme stress, trauma, or adversity—such as abuse, neglect, loss, a loved one's illness, homelessness, or a natural disaster—you may struggle with intense emotions as a result. The good news is you can move past toxic stress, let go of fear and anger, and build resilience and well-being.

This engaging workbook offers powerful skills to help you overcome the effects of trauma and adversity—and thrive. You'll learn all about how your mind and body respond to stress, how to identify emotional triggers, and how to stay grounded when your life feels too big to handle. If you're struggling with the effects of toxic stress, you should know that you are not alone, and there is nothing to be ashamed of. With this workbook, you can start moving through your trauma and toward the life you want.

LET THIS WORKBOOK GUIDE YOU TO:

* Cultivate confidence and self-compassion

* Move past self-harming behaviors
* Manage intense thoughts and feelings
* Find inner calm when you need it most

"Hope and healing are just moments away in this fabulous manual to move from struggling with trauma to living freely and fully with strength and joy."
—DANIEL J. SIEGEL, MD, *New York Times* bestselling author of *Brainstorm*